THE *REALITY* OF MYTH

SECOND EDITION

JOHN HILARY MARTIN

SOLAS PRESS
ANTIOCH
2012

Permissions Dept.
SOLAS Press
2420 Sand Creek Rd. STE C1 #258
Brentwood CA 94513   USA

http://www.solaspress.com. E-mail info@solaspress.com

Library of Congress Catalogued the First Edition as follows:
Martin, John Hilary 1929-

The reality of myth / by John Hilary Martin.
p. cm.
Includes bibliographical references (p)
ISBN 1-893426-99-8 (pbk)
Myth. I. Title

BL311 .M345 2001
291 . 1'3—dc21

2001042623

ISBN 978-1-893426-95-5

DEDICATION

To the people of Wadeye Australia and my mentors and students who, over the years, have labored with me on these ideas.

JHM

PREFACE

What is the relationship of myth to reality? The genesis of the ideas connected with this question occurred to me when I was Scholar in Residence at John XXIII College. In 1993, Ian Waite, the Master of the College, invited me to lecture on a fitting question for the Year of the Indigenous Person. The subject of myth and ritual and how they bring about our perception of reality immediately came to mind. The topic is a perennial one but that, of course, does not mean any consensus has been reached.

Another seminal event for me was the Mabo decision. In Australia in 1992 the Justices of the High Court of Australia attempted to right wrongs which had been perpetrated during the founding of the nation. The Mabo decision of the court affirmed land rights that had been denied to Aboriginal Australians.

The wrongs stemmed in large measure from the new settlers failure to understand the Aboriginal Australians attachment to their land. Their attachment to land was always a function of the Dreaming. The Dreaming is a complex system of myths and rituals, and multilevel symbolism. It seemed appropriate then, to tie notions of the Dreaming to daily living.

It is with pleasure I express my gratitude both to Ian Waite, the Master of John XXIII College, for his support of my lecture series and to the Indigenous Australians who inspired me with regard to myth and ritual.

The lectures series was written at a time when I was reading through the papers of W. E. H. Stanner, the Australian

v

anthropologist. I want to thank most especially his wife, Mrs. P. Stanner, who graciously gave me permission to read his valuable material. W. E. H. Stanner was well liked among the communities he studied, and is remembered as one of the first to turn a sympathetic ear toward the religion of the indigenous people of Australia. I would be pleased if some of his insights had rubbed off on me in the writing of these pages. I also thank those at the Australian Institute of Aboriginal and Torres Strait Islander Studies for their help with the project.

I am indebted to colleagues too numerous to mention who have helped me sift and strengthen my ideas. In particular I am indebted to Antoninus Wall and Gavin Colvert who snatched time from their busy schedules to read and comment on the entire manuscript. Last, but not least, I am grateful to Dominic Colvert my editor at SOLAS Press. He has made many substantive suggestions for improvement.

In writing on these arcane topics it is alas inevitable that there will be some lack of clarity, miscommunications, errors of interpretation, and so on. For any deficiencies I retain full responsibility.

JOHN HILARY MARTIN

Camberwell Victoria

December 2000

CONTENTS

FOREWORD

How can mythology best be studied and understood? When Wendy Doniger, Hilary Martin and I were together on the faculty in comparative religion at the Graduate Theological Union, Berkeley, a lively discussion ensued over just this topic, and eventually it was Doniger who settled the matter. There was "a myth of methodology in the study of mythology," she asserted. Instead of a single interpretation Doniger recommended a toolbox approach. Theories were fine, she thought, as long as you did not confuse them with truth: they were simply conceptual tools to help in translating the meanings from other people and other times into language and images that make sense to us.

The metaphor of translation is apt. It suggests that there is no one correct way of interpreting mythology, nor one right way of perceiving truth. In trying to understand myths, we are simply translating, and perhaps attempting to recreate, the meanings transported from other people's social and historical contexts into our own. When we translate we do not pretend that we are enunciating the real meaning of words, or that our way of saying them is truer than the original language.

Like translation, the study of myth is nonjudgmental. In making sense of a myth we can happily ignore the issue of whether our way of explaining it or theirs is truer, or whether there is in fact an objective and permanent reality in the world. That is something for scientists to debate.

Instead, mythology deals with something of far more practical importance: perceptions of reality. Although the images of mythology — like language — are by nature changing and particular, they contain meanings that outlive their temporality. Hence the reality that myths point towards is in many ways more enduring than the mythic reality that we feel so secure about in our everyday world.

This is the theme that Hilary Martin explores in this useful and interesting book. Focusing on the Australian Aboriginal material that he knows so well, Martin compares the rich mythology of this culture with images from the Native North American tradition and the Bible. He uses a toolbox approach in utilizing a variety of methods — philosophical, anthropological, literary, and theological — to explore the way that the meanings in mythology endure and reveal insights about reality that are significant in the present day.

Martin's theological insights and biblical references are particularly useful in allowing readers from a Christian background to understand the relevance of indigenous traditions to enduring matters of meaning and faith. This approach is a timely one, since in a global world, issues of faith and meaning, myth and reality, are no longer forged in a vacuum. The globalization of culture forces one to raise these questions in multicultural and multi-religious contexts.

Increasingly all of the world's religious traditions are the inheritance of everyone on the planet. In that sense, understanding the significance of Australian Aboriginal and Native American mythology is to uncover layers of our own global cultural heritage. In this book, Hilary Martin helps us do this on several levels: he demonstrates the value of comparative scholarship not only for cross-cultural understanding but also for personal enrichment and meaning in a global age.

MARK JUERGENSMEYER

Santa Barbara, California

August 2001

THE *REALITY* OF MYTH

CHAPTER I

STORIES ABOUT HIGHER TRUTH

Myths have a timeless value. But this claim seems pretentious to some minds. They feel myths are all right 'in their own way' because they help primitive pre-historical people celebrate the changeless rhythms of their universe — which is really all they have! They think myths are certainly not for people who have progressed beyond the world of nature and live with a consciousness of human history.

Of course, there is no reason to place myth over and against history and physical reality as if myths were some kind of dark mental phenomena that vanished in the light of day. What passes for reality is hardly as solid as myth. Reality is constantly changing and presents a new face every day. Who could live in the shoes of their great-grandparents or even in the shoes of their parents?

Reality presents a continuous stream of new facts. Without myths to digest these facts they leave only a welter of confusion in their wake. Myth embodies the subjective desires for meaning and permanence that drive our activities. Myth and reality, the subjective and objective, must form in each of us a unified whole if our personal and communal life is to be deal with successfully.

Our aim will be to investigate how myth and reality work together. First we must examine what is myth, and distinguish secular myth from religious myth. This is no easy task since the word *myth* is used in many ways and in many languages. Ultimately our best understanding will come from an examination of mythic stories. The examples selected here are drawn from the Bible, North American mythology, and the Dreaming of the Aboriginal Australian.

Having gained an awareness of myth we will show how much mythic insight dominates our approach to history — history as an account of reality. Conversely we will show there is much history in primitive myths. When examining history we will see that our intuitive and reflective understanding of the world is much more than an accumulation of historical facts.

We will also find that ritual is an essential part of a theory of history. It is through ritual that meaning is inculcated and traditions are brought into the present.

One of the claims put forward for myths is that they enable us to talk about what would otherwise be beyond our understanding. Through symbolism they introduce us to a supra-sensible world using imagery drawn from the world of everyday experience.

We will show that through symbolism our ideals of the transcendental can be grounded in reality. While there is mystery and considerable complexity attached to interpreting symbols, this will be at once the most basic as well as the most interesting and illuminating part of our investigation of the reality of myth.

Secular and Religious Myths

Philosophers, psychologists, linguists and sociologists, as well as theologians and historians of religion, have continually labored over what they mean by myth. Scholars have also made great efforts to clarify the Australian Aborigines notion of the Dreaming. As G. S. Kirk has prudently remarked, "General theories of myth and ritual are no easy matter."[1] Deborah Rose warns that, "Aboriginal people use the term the Dreaming to refer to a wide range of concepts and entities which are not all covered by the same term in their own languages."[2]

In inquiring into myth and the Dreaming, let us turn first to ancient mythology. The process of definition and redefinition ongoing in academic circles shows that *myth* is not a very precise term. The content of myths may very well overlap with folk tales, sagas or legends. The large body of writing coming from so many different disciplines should also alert us to the fact that myth and myth-making are highly complex phenomena and that myths make an impact on our character and personality in a variety of ways. Later when we analyze myths that are bound together with rituals we will find that their complexity and impact on us is even greater.

In part we use myths because the human intellect is capable of reaching beyond ordinary experience. We can move beyond scientific analyses when investigating existence. This quest leads us to look into a mysterious part of our lives that raises questions like: where did I come from? why am I here? and what about the afterlife?

Myths are often regarded in a vague way as religious phenomena. The minimalist definition given by E. B. Tylor in the 19th century that myths were, 'stories about the gods' has some value.[3] Ernst Cassirer, after analyzing thoughts of the German Romantics felt that all myths were at least potentially religious phenomena.[4] Cassirer's judgment was colored by considerations derived from the epistemology of Friedrich von Schelling and Georg Hegel and not from an empirical analysis of myths themselves.[5] Kirk gives a more sensible answer to the question, 'are myths sacred stories or not?' He suggests the narratives can be about sacred events, folklore tales, entertainment, and the like; and that they are always in the form of a story. The myths treat the stories in a particular way and produce specific effects on the psyche.[6]

While nineteenth century theorists may have been comfortable with the idea that all myths were at root covert histories of the gods of old, nowadays myth-like tales about folk heroes and heroines attract more attention. Those tales and quasi-rituals concerned with political and sports figures have a decidedly secular ring to them and have little obvious connection with religion.

The mystical goodness that clung to the reputation of President John Kennedy in the United States following his assassination in 1963; or the aura of being a wounded hero that surrounding Prime Minister Gough Whitlam in Australia after his abrupt dismissal in 1975 from office can be regarded as examples of secular myths. Political figures are not the only ones given a mythical stature larger than life. Examples of modern persons with mythical stature, such as Martin Luther King and Mother Teresa of Calcutta, could be multiplied.

We can draw up a 'rough and ready' outline of the secular myth-making process. The myth making begins with a popular and charismatic figure. In stories about them the individual's faults and failings are glossed over. Their virtues and positive accomplishments are spoken of in glowing and appealing terms until the person attains heroic status, and his or her message seems to speak the wisdom of the ages. The result is, of course, not history, and should not be accepted as such. It is a secular myth!

But do we need to go to the great and the powerful to find instances of mythologizing? We may have possibly witnessed it ourselves. Imagine a unit as small as a family inventing a myth to justify its actions and then even coming to believe it. "Why in the world," a family member may be asked, "did you move out of your home in the old neighborhood near the center of the town and move to that distant suburb with its insufferably long commute?" Imagine the reply as follows. "We moved to the suburbs because our folks originally came from a farming background. Dad wanted to work on the bit of land in the garden and mother loves flowers. And would you guess when the agent showed us the new house we found a lucky penny on the front path! You can't pass up lucky pennies, can you?" Behind the charmingly arranged phrases lies other reasons, the real reasons for the family move. They moved because property taxes in town were getting too high, the local schools were poor, and the complexion of the old neighborhood was changing. The story told by the family to cover the gap between the respectable and the real reasons for moving was a myth.

In all likelihood, it will be the more poetic reasons for the move that the family will eventually remember. They will conveniently forget that their story was constructed to gloss over their real motivation. Myths are like that! Myths recalibrate events and draw a picture of life, as it ideally should be rather than how it actually was.

Religious texts, like the Bible, are not entirely free of mythologizing of this type. For example, the long lament made by David because he had cut the hem of King Saul's cloak when he had him at his mercy in the cave near Engedi, betrays something of this.[7] David had shown more than average restraint in not killing King Saul outright when he blundered into the cave where David had been hiding. Instead, we are told,

David merely surreptitiously cut a piece off the edge of Saul's garment so that Saul would discover later how much danger he had been in. When the story is retold in Scripture, David is presented as weeping and worrying about presuming to have so much as touched Saul, because Saul was the Lord's anointed. David's sorrow and remorse about touching Saul is excessive. It is, of course, an excellent club to instill the rule that it is very wicked to attempt any sort of violence against the Lord's anointed ones — such as King David's royal successors. David's supposed sorrow is the official interpretation of the events. Reading between the lines, it looks very much like an opportunistic rationalization. Bible scholars assure us, that precisely because falsity lies so close to the surface, David's lament is doubtless a later gloss added for political reasons.

With secular myths — such as the Kennedy and the Whitlam legends, or the story put out by our humble family as they joined the flight to the suburbs — the truth of the matter can be discovered. At least it can be shrewdly surmised with a little investigation. Witness the demythologizing going on in biographies and in television documentaries about President Kennedy. Even the mythical aspects of David's lament can be punctured when the hermeneutics of suspicion has done its work. In all the above instances myth takes the form of rearranging material to make a point. And, we might add, the makers of the myth are themselves often well aware of the rearrangements. If rearranging things to tell a vivid story is what is meant by myth, then, the term can obviously cover secular, non-religious material.

It is important then to try to isolate the special character of religious myths. If myths can be secular, if even biblical narratives can have a secular side to them, what then makes a myth religious? Is the difference simply a matter that the content is about gods?

It is possible to examine religious myths as if they were simple stories whose material had been rearranged to illustrate some point about religion. But this is to reduce religious myths to something they are not. The concern of religious myths, unlike their secular counterparts, is not with rearranging material that is quite obvious in order to make an ethical or political point. Religious myths may do that along the way, but their primary purpose is to introduce us to things that are not known and open to ordinary inspection. Religious myths endeavor to speak about the mystery of God and divine activities. They try to answer questions that have been moral conundrums over the ages.

Religious myths express, albeit in an imperfect way, what cannot be seen, what cannot be known by ordinary canons of experience. For example, they report history when no witnesses were present; they confidently predict the future; they see into the hidden motives of men and women. As Saint John's Gospel succinctly puts it, "No one has ever seen God; the only Son, who is in the bosom of the Father, he has made him known."[8] Because they do not appeal to ordinary experience, they employ many symbols. Because they touch on mystery, the answers that religious myths give are rarely the clear and simple answers we would like to hear.

The History of Myth

As suggested earlier, the study of myth continues to be attractive. Unfortunately lengthy discussions about the meaning of myths have been inconclusive, and we have been left with a somewhat fluid terminology. Fortunately, the actuality of myths has been more stable than the terminology.

This is not the place for a full discussion but a brief overview will be useful.

In Greek the term muthos originally meant simply a rumor, something one was told. Initially neither truth nor falsity was implied, but muthos soon was regarded as the likely story, as distinct from the logos that was the true account. Myth then merged into fable, that is, stories that were freely invented to entertain audiences and to illustrate some moral truth. This is the way Aristotle thought of them.[9]

Since fables, in this sense, were not the best way of imparting higher forms of knowledge it was an easy step to think of them as 'light weight' and unworthy of rigorous analysis. In later Greek usage they were definitely not true accounts and came to be regarded as deceptive and erroneous, perhaps even superstitions.

Muthos are referred to in the New Testament in the later letters of Saint Paul. He is wary of studying such fabulous stories and genealogies because they merely nourish idle curiosity when one should be paying attention to sound doctrine and to living a good life. But Paul seems to have Jewish stories and genealogies, possibly the apocrypha, in mind and not the classical pagan literature.

Medieval commentators on Scripture were well aware of myths, but they had learned to use them. Medieval society in general made frequent use of rituals, stories, and symbolism in presenting Christianity. Thomas Aquinas, whose forte was in logical forms of thought, nevertheless found a place for fables. He said fables that were composed of *miris* (marvelous events) were intended to lead people to acquire virtue and avoid vice. He thought simple people are better instructed through representations than through reasoning. Thomas interpreted

Paul's warning as being only against the excessive use of the myth form, not as an outright attack on them. He reasoned that myths have a certain truth-value that reaches beyond that derived from mere observation of the facts of our lived experience. They become vain stories only when they present the truth in impossible ways and they become inept stories when they present it in inappropriate ways.[10] Myths are to be used, but with caution!

Polemic debates during the Protestant and Catholic Reformations generated a literalist approach to Scripture. Allegorical and symbolic arguments were put very much in the background. The venerable medieval practice of finding moral, historical, and allegorical levels of meaning in Scriptural texts was called into question or discarded. The climate of hermeneutics of that time was openly hostile to myth and mythologizing tendencies. The word myth became associated with infidelity.

A Renewal of Interest in Myth

In the early nineteenth century the term myth made a re-appearance in theological literature in connection with the study of Greek and Roman mythology.[11] By then the medieval position had long been forgotten. The stories derived from classical mythology were clearly false stories since they were about the non-existent gods of Homeric polytheism. In this sense there obviously could be no myths in the Bible.

It could hardly be denied, however, that there were many stories in the Bible that looked very much like the myths in other religions. It was hard to deny that pagan myths dressed in literary forms of the ancient Middle East, and in a truncated and vague form could be found in Scripture. Some argued that despite the appearances, myths, at least complete myths, could not be found in the Bible; because its monotheism is hostile to them. Because of its monotheistic tradition Bible stories that have a mythic format are different from those in classical mythology. Following the definition of E. B. Tylor that myths are 'stories of the gods,' belief in at least two gods would be essential. Furthermore, Biblical stories lay claim to a central core of historical truth while the Greek and Roman mythologies recounted in the 19th century did not.

Can it be asserted that pagan myths invariably lay no claim to historical content? Australian Aboriginal Elders, who in the Dreaming recite sacred stories about ancestral beings who formed and shaped the land, believe they are talking about events that have actually taken place. Therefore it becomes necessary to reexamine the argument that the Bible lacks myths because of its claim, a unique claim it is often said, to be an historical account.

Mythic Forms in Major Religions

The Christian story can be described as a myth cycle with major moments that encapsulate its history. They are:

(a) Creation of the universe.

(b) The Fall of humanity from its original relation to God.

(c) The Incarnation, and the atonement by Jesus Christ.

(d) The bodily Resurrection of Christ, and the final resurrection and judgment of humanity on the Last Day.

All these elements with the exception of the Incarnation and atoning work of Christ fall easily into the category of myth. It is true that the Incarnation and the work of Christ fall within human history, but they embrace mythical aspects as well. There are historical sources for the events of Jesus Christ's life in Palestine and his prophetic works. But while their actuality is historical their meaning is ultimately cast in terms of myth.

The pattern also appears in Judaism. Its story is of Creation, the Fall of the first man and woman, the calling of the Chosen People, and their eternal destiny culminating in the times of the Messiah. Islam can be described using a similar cycle of events where one of the moments is the call of the Prophet Mohammed, the seal of the prophets. In Mahayana Buddhism the Lord Buddha is a historical person about whom mythic stories, that is, stories beyond historical scrutiny, have been woven.

How is it appropriate to use the term myth in the context of these religions and particularly in reference to the Christian cycle? Is myth to be reserved just for those aspects of the stories that do not have solid historical roots? If this were the case the term myth would express a non-historical framework into which historical events were inserted. While such an insertion is possible, to do so it risks being arbitrary and open to subjective evaluations.

Alternately it is possible to use the term myth to express a historical point of view throughout all the elements of the cycle. The entire Christian cycle, with the exception of Judgment Day, can be viewed as made of historical/ontological events. Admittedly they are dressed up in poetic language when presented in Scripture. In this view of things, the story of creation told in Genesis tells of the actual production of the world by a single divine actor at a point in time; the fall of humanity is a record of the collapse of human integrity illustrated by actual events.

For those who wish to see a divine force moving and shaping the cosmos it is possible to regard the four divisions of the Christian cycle as a myth with stories of events that move between time and eternity. They tell of God's actions in relation to human beings that are actually on going, and so are historical or at least ontological. These events stand outside of normal historical scrutiny since they cannot be tested by ordinary scientific approaches. Their truth stands or falls on the acceptance of myth.

For those who wish to consider only tangible human experience and want to avoid intruding transcendental or faith elements into a study of history myths can still have power. They can sum up and promote the culture of a community. This is essentially the position of authors like Gordon Kaufman.[12] He speaks of the Fall of humanity as an event occurring over many centuries as human free will cut into the boundaries established by the Creator. In this view myth is history taking place over a period of time. Myth may be called forth to interpret past events, but myth has become little more than a word to describe the historical process. In this view, myths while perhaps not false, in reality lose any independent meaning or value.

In the 20th century myths began to be treated more positively. They came to be viewed as the universal yearnings of humanity from the archetypes in the individual unconscious or the collective unconscious of the human race. Myths contained values that are perennial and universal! In consequence, myth-like stories were thought worth examining because they expressed a primitive revelation that had been given to all or gained by all in the course of human history. Mythic stories though complex and not proceeding in a straightforward literal manner had risen from being false stories, or essentially meaningless ones, to become repositories of hidden higher truth.

CHAPTER II

THE ORIGIN MYTHS

I will now proceed in an inductive fashion to examine religious myths. The following three examples tell of the formation of the world. The first is an Indian story from North America; the second is the Genesis story from the Bible, coming from the ancient Near East; the third is a Dreaming story from the Central Australian Desert. Each of these is part of a cycle of myths which give a fuller account of a people. While 'origin narratives' may not be the most crucial part of these accounts they help orient the other stories of the cycle.

The Maidu Account of the Origins of the World

The Maidu are an Indian people living in a inland area of Northern California near Mount Lassen. It would be more precise to call this a myth of the formation of the earth rather than a creation story, since it tells about a number of primal beings with muted creator roles. A Maidu elder related the story in English to members of the Huntington California Expedition in 1902.

The story had been told and retold among Maidu people from time immemorial. Like all such narratives in an oral tradition it has been arranged and adapted, in the retelling, to fit the audience at hand. By 1902 many of a storytellers' listeners would be people with Christian backgrounds so it would not be surprising if echoes of Biblical decor have found their way into the narrative.

The Maidu story has characteristics that are similar to stories from the Dreaming told by Australian Aborigines. It would, however, be inaccurate to label this myth as a story from the Dreaming. This story cycle does not, as in the case of Australian Aboriginal stories, tell of the formation of a specific land, nor does it precisely associate the Maidu society with any particular land or ancestor. It should be noted that Native American Peoples do not have a word equivalent to the Dreaming.

The Maidu people of California had a loose tribal organization with no visible expression of totemism. Their main occupation was hunting and gathering in a rich semi-forested area.

Tribal life was not uncomfortable or impoverished. Families lived in well-built circular lodges 12 feet to 15 feet in diameter. The roof, which was conical in shape, had an opening at the top which served as a smoke hole, and perhaps gave access to the sky. There was one small, low door near the ground requiring everyone, in a symbolic action, to crawl into the lodge on hands and knees.

Only two rites seemed to have had major importance — an annual burning of possessions and an 'initiation' ceremony for boys at puberty. The burning ceremony was performed to honor and remember the dead, especially those who had died in recent years. The initiation ceremony was for eligible boys after careful consultation with the elders. Initiation is perhaps not the best title for this Maidu rite since only some boys were selected. Those initiated became *yeponi* — members of a secret society — and were held in honor and looked up to.

The creation myth reported here has points of connection with the stories of the Wintum and Yana Indian groups located nearby in the Shasta and Pit River areas. Indeed the Maidu story of an animal diving for earth was one that was widely distributed over North America. For example, the Algonquin in the northeastern part of the continent have a similar story using a different species of animal. All these stories speak of the first formation of the earth. It should be noted however, that some Indian tribes in Southern California spoke of God simply thinking the world into existence from a void — so creation stories were also present.[13]

According to the Maidu:[14]

In the beginning there was no sun, no moon, no stars. All was dark, and everywhere there was only water. A raft came floating on the water. It came from the North and in it were two persons — Turtle (Anosma) and the Father-of-the-Secret-Society (Peheipe).[15] The stream flowed very rapidly. Then from the sky a rope of feathers (*pokelma*) was let down, and down it came the Earth-Initiate. When he reached the end of the rope, he tied it to the bow of the raft and stepped in. His face was covered and was never seen, but his body shone like the sun. He sat down and for a long time said nothing.

At last Turtle said, "Where do you come from?"

And Earth-Initiate answered, "I come from above."

Then Turtle said, "Brother can you not make for me some good dry land, so that I may sometimes come up out of the water?" Then he asked another time, "Are there going to be any people in the world?"

Earth-Initiate thought for a while, then said, "Yes."

Turtle asked, "How long before you are going to make people?"

Earth-Initiate replied, "I don't know. You want to have some dry land: well how am I going to get any earth to make it?"

Turtle answered, "If you will tie a rock about my left arm, I'll dive for some."

Earth-Initiate did as Turtle asked, and then, reaching around took the end of a rope from somewhere and tied it to Turtle. (When Earth-Initiate came to the raft, there was no rope there: he just reached out and found one.)

Turtle said, "If the rope is not long enough, I'll jerk it once, and you must haul me up; if it is long enough, I'll give two jerks, and then you must pull me up quickly as I shall have all the earth that I can carry."

Just as Turtle went over the side of the boat the Father-of-the-Secret-Society began to shout loudly.

Turtle was gone a long time. He was gone six years; and when he came up he was covered with green slime, he had been down so long. When he reached the top of the water the only earth he had was a very little under his nails: the rest had all washed away. Earth-Initiate took with his right hand a stone knife from under his left armpit and carefully scraped the earth out from under Turtle's nails. He put the earth in the palm of his hand and rolled it about till it was round; it was as large as a small pebble. He laid it in the stern of the raft. By and by he went to look at it: it had not grown at all. The third time he went to look at it, it had grown so that it could be spanned by the arms. The fourth time he looked, it was as big as the world, the raft was aground, and all around were mountains as far as he could see. The raft came ashore at Tádoiko, and the place can be seen today.

What shall we make of this story? It might be described as a creation narrative with Earth-Initiate as the creator figure. However, as already noted, it would be better to describe it as a formation story. There is the Father-of-the Secret-Society who shouts out loudly both here and later on at other key points in the story, which we have not been able to include here. There is a third figure, Turtle, who announces that he wants a rock tied to his left arm before he goes over the side for six years to search for land to multiply. He manages to bring up a little bit from the bottom of the sea — so the earth is primordial. Finally there is the mundane reality of Tádoiko, a place that you can see to this day if you know where to look.

We have an apparent history and possible scientific discussion, but we are intuitively aware even at the first reading that the story is designed to tell more than meets the eye. The world of Anosma, Peheipe and Earth-Initiate is hardly a world of science or engineering. Turtle was gone for six years and when he came up he was covered with green slime, but that is a pretended fact imitating a human observation. The story transports us to a place where all mundane questions and answers can be suspended. Listeners soon find that they must be comfortable in a world where extraordinary events occur, and where the narrator without any apparent embarrassment puts incomplete and even inconsistent descriptions of them forward. They are in a realm of fluid thought with numerous non-sequiturs.

As we pursue the Maidu story further we find a querulous Turtle still complaining:

"I can't stay in the dark all the time. Can't you make a light, so that I can see?"

Earth-Initiate replied, "Let us get out of the raft, and then we will see what we can do."

So all three got out.

Then the Earth-Initiate said, "Look that way, to the east! I am going to tell my sister to come up"

Then it began to grow light, and day began to break; then the Father-of-the-Secret-Society began to shout loudly, and the sun came up.

"Which way is the sun to travel," Turtle asked?

Earth-Initiate answered, "I'll tell her to go this way and go down there."

After the sun went down the Father-of-the-Secret-Society began to cry and shout again, and it grew very dark.

Earth-Initiate said, "I'll tell my brother to come up"

Then the moon rose.

Then Earth-Initiate asked Turtle and The-Father-of-the-Secret-Society, "How do you like it"

And they both answered, "It is very good."

Turtle's demands are, of course, quite inconsistent. The Earth-Initiate was described as radiant and a source of light as he sat in the raft before Turtle began his dive. But this story, like so many other religious myths has no problems with inconsistency, nor for that matter is it concerned with fussy, pettifogging details about Turtle as a person. What is important to the story is Turtle's place in the action. It is he who dives to the bottom of the sea to get land for the Earth-Initiate to multiply.

The Story in Genesis

In the origin story from the Bible the mythic patterns appear again. Although the first chapter of Genesis opens with an origin story it is by no means the oldest part of the book. It was probably set down in its present form after the exile of the Jews from Judea to Babylon in 587 BC. This story too had been told and retold, and was borrowed in part from an earlier mythology of the Middle East.[16]

According to Genesis:[17]

> In the beginning God created the heavens and the earth. The earth was without form and void, and darkness was upon the face of the deep; and the Spirit of God was moving over the face of the waters. And God said, "Let there be light"; and there was light. And God saw that the light was good; and God separated the light from the darkness. God called the light Day, and the darkness he called Night. And there was evening and there was morning, one day.

The story goes on to discuss the work of the second and third days. That work involves a division of the waters into those

19

above and below, and the formation of the vault of heaven, or rather the dome forming the sky.

On the forth day new lights are made for the sky. Dry land, separated from the sea, is made to appear at God's command. After that, the land is then called upon to bring forth vegetation of all sorts.

> And God said, "Let there be lights in the firmament of the heavens to separate the day from the night; and let them be for signs and for seasons and for days and years, and let them be lights in the firmament of the heavens to give light upon the earth." And it was so. And God made the two great lights, the greater light to rule the day, and the lesser light to rule the night; he made the stars also. And God set them in the firmament of the heavens to give light upon the earth, to rule over the day and over the night, and to separate the light from the darkness. And God saw that it was good. And there was evening and there was morning, a fourth day.[18]

On the fifth day the waters are allowed to teem with an abundance of living creatures and birds populate the sky. They are told to, "Be fruitful and multiply...on the earth."[19]

On the sixth day the earth is invited to, "Bring forth cattle and creeping and beasts of the earth according to their kinds." The invitations to the sea and the earth to be fruitful can be interpreted as simply a literary flourish; but the more likely purpose is to emphasize that it is God who actually initiates everything that comes to be. On this sixth and final day of creation God created human beings:

> Let us make man in our image, and after our likeness; and let them have dominion over the fish of

the sea, and over the birds of the air, and over the cattle and over all the earth ... So God created man in his own image, in the image of God he created him; male and female he created them.[20]

The original couple were blessed and told to, "Be fruitful and multiply, to fill the earth and to subdue it." They were explicitly given dominion over all living creatures whether in the sea, the sky or on the earth.[21]

At length, on the seventh day God, "Rested from all his work which he had he had done ... and saw how good it all was."

In the Genesis account the constant repetition of the phrase "God saw how good it was" makes it clear that all creation is good and that the ordering of all the works of creation is good as well. Although nothing is explicitly said, we are left with the distinct impression that position, arrangement, separation and order are quite important values in the Divine scheme of things. This is no doubt appropriate since Genesis is the preface to the Torah the book of the Law.

In Genesis we come upon mild contradictions, disruptions, and highlighting in service of its agenda of the sort we saw in the Maidu story. Great emphasis is placed on the creation of light in Genesis. It is God's first activity, and it came forth at his command. He separates it from the darkness so that it becomes possible to speak of a first day. This action is significant, presented dramatically and not the sort of thing that is likely to be forgotten. But, as in the Maidu story, it seems to be forgotten almost at once. Although God has already said, "Let there be light" lights are created in the dome of the sky. Taken out of the mythical context these two descriptions would require some justification. They could be considered as simple contradictions of a forgetful author, or as anachronisms, or as the conflation of two separate stories sewn together in a 'ham handed' way.

These descriptions present no difficulty at all, however, in a mythical landscape. Such discontinuities are commonplace for those who think in terms of myth. As the schoolmen of the Middle Ages noted, disembodied light and the visible light of the sun can, of course, be regarded as two separate entities entitled to a separate creation by God.

The story can be treated as if it were stubborn or esoteric science, but the ensuing complications are enormous and the results usually unsatisfactory. The pages of patristic, medieval and even modern biblical exegesis are littered with futile attempts to force Genesis to make historical or scientific sense.

Upon hearing a myth ordinary listeners realize it can say more than one thing. Genesis may seem to say the heavens-and-the-earth in the first instance lay about as a formless wasteland, a dark abyss of wind-swept waters. On the other hand, it can seem to say the heavens-and the-earth came forth directly from God's creative hand. The context must supply meaning!

By means of layered imagery and apparent inconsistency, repetition and discontinuity, difficult concepts like non-existence, effortless multiplication of objects, the conditions of the earth as it was formed, are gradually made, if not understandable, at least accessible.

The Genesis story, as well as the Maidu narrative, and so many other creation stories, invite us to suspend normal historical and scientific curiosity because they have something more important to say. We are invited to disengage our thoughts and our concerns about the ordinary pattern of life, suspend our disbelief and listen to what they are saying. Myths

22

attempt to tell us truths that cannot be known in any other way.

Through myth we learn about the way the cosmos unfolds. In Genesis the God who produced light acts alone. As the story unfolds God is the solitary actor who shapes and forms all that comes to be. There is no need, nor any room, for a second principle to assist with creation. One by one the animals are all presented by God to Adam for him to name, but only to name. It is God who has made them all. God alone is without father or mother; without family, spouse, or helper.

Arrernte Story of Creation

The following is an origin story from the Arrernte (Arunta, Aranda), an aboriginal people who live southeast of Alice Springs in central Australia. This story was told to Spencer and Gillen — and recast by Mircea Eliade.[22] It is a fragment of a long series or cycle of myths of the Achilpa (Tjilpa), a sub-group of the Arrernte.

According to the traditions of the Achilpa:[23]

...the ancestral figures the Nambakula arose from nowhere (out of nothing) far to the South. Traveling north from his camp at Lamburkna one established a Dreaming track. As he went he shaped the mountains, rivers, and produced all sorts of plants and animals. He also brought forth the *kuruna* (spirit children) which were inside his body. He made the *tjurungas* which imaged the things he was making and made sacred store houses to keep them in. This was before any human beings existed. ...the *kuruna* came out of the cave to become the first Achilpa men....

In this Dreaming story an ancestral being, whose origin is unknown, comes upon the land to shape all the geographical features of the Arrernte landscape and to populate it with all the plants and animals of the area. Before Nambakula's coming the area was formless and indefinite without rivers, seas, mountains or physical features of any kind. The Nambakula was just one of the many creative beings who made a trek across the Continent during the period known as the alchera,[24] or the Dreaming.

The work of the Dreaming ancestors formed the Australian landscape as it is; and probably in the minds of Aborigines, the way it should remain. The origin stories of the different tribes of Australia insist on many ancestral beings. These stories foster a polycentered understanding of creation since the interactions of the ancestors do not appear to have proceeded in any particularly coordinated manner.

The action of forming and shaping the land and populating it with plant and animal life is emphasized in this myth. Australian Aboriginal origin myths, focus most of their attention on the land itself leaving aside for the most part references to sky or water. The land and the power of ancestral figures residing in the land is of central significance. Although a dominant and an authoritative figure, the Nambakula does not create the land. Land is primordial. It existed before him, or at least was contemporaneous with him, and he requires land to work out the ordering of creation.

Chapter III

MYTH AND DREAMING

The origin myths tell us authoritatively and without guesswork what we could not otherwise know. Where did earth and land come from? The Maidu story answers that by dramatically describing Turtle's leap over the side of the raft and dive to the bottom of the sea in search of soil so the Earth-Initiate can construct the world. Myths inform us about the state of the world at its beginning when there were no witnesses to record what was going on. They talk about mysterious realities such as: how the first sun came up, how men and women arose on the earth, how men found their first stable foods.

While these myths have much to say about the earth, the cosmos, and God; they cannot be relied upon for specific information. They will not enlighten the reader directly about primitive science, tribal histories or ancient memories of the race. Such myths are, however, an essential element of everyone's daily experiences. It will be useful to review the three origin myths to see what information they give and how they work to affect their listeners.

Suspension of Normal Judgment

At the beginning of the Maidu story two figures are discovered in a raft traveling south. As they drift along, a rope of feathers suddenly appears. Then, a third figure, Earth-Initiate enters the raft and sits down after cautiously tying the rope to the bow of the raft. Tying the rope is apparently an event important enough to be mentioned, although nothing is ever made of it. As the story unfolds, much continues to be left unexplained. Characters, such as Earth-Initiate, enter abruptly; and events occur without preparation, as when the hitherto passive Father-of-the-Secret-Society begins to shout loudly. Through it all the narrators do not tarry to give conventional explanations.

The raft's occupants simply came from the North. How long the journey from the beginning might have been, what else might be in the North is 'off stage' and is deliberately left 'off stage' throughout the story. A rope of feathers drops from above! Was the place above also filled with water? Is it a world that is a double of our own? We are never told, but are simply left with an inchoate awareness that there might be some other reality beyond the boat and the stream. Apropos of nothing in particular, we are told that the water on which the raft was traveling was running very swiftly. Is this stream a current in an ocean, or is it a river between two hidden banks? We will never know, nor should we even want to know. To impart information of this kind is not the purpose of a myth. Mood is more important.

When the sudden shouting by the Father-of-the-Secret-Society first breaks into the story listeners are left with an uneasy feeling that this might be important, but they are left hanging. Their suspicion is confirmed since the Father-of-the-Secret-Society does the same thing when various things happen at other points in the story. It could be connected with the secret society of tribal initiates; but precisely why is not explained.

Various narrative devices reinforce mood. There are dramatic repetitions, disruptions, irrelevant remarks, all of which serve to emphasize the special character of selected events.

The plot of the story is spare and lacking in explanations. When the need for some land comes up Turtle simply volunteers to get some by diving to the bottom of the water. The soil he brings back gradually extends itself after being handled by Earth-Initiate. In mythical landscapes loose ends like these are quietly allowed to remain as loose ends. Listeners are not given scientific information; rather they are invited to suspend scientific judgments. Intuitively they are aware that no Maidu tribesman ever saw earth grow and expand by itself.

The underlying climate of all three myths is that we should not be surprised at anything that happens. Story segments are separated, divided and linked together so that what looks like history is presented without historical links. Normal judgments, both historical and scientific, must be suspended, so myths can tell us what we could not otherwise know. They communicate a mystery and tell about the reality that supports the phenomenal world.

Multiple Levels of Meaning

The intriguing beauty of these tales is their ability to affect their hearers at many levels at once. They simultaneously engage emotions, prick curiosity, raise expectations and recall the past — even a past not consciously perceived. Before the Genesis story about the temptation of Adam and Eve in the Garden of Eden is completed it is intuitively clear that they will indeed eat the fruit that was forbidden to them. This is because no adult and few children come to a myth without some remembrance of a communal past.

27

Style is used to reinforce the effects of these myths. Shouting by the Father-of-the-Secret-Society sets up expectations that condition the psyche. As in other fables formal phrases are repeated. Often the formal phrases in fables, such as "I'll huff and puff and blow your house down," are repeated three times. It is perhaps for this reason that Earth-Initiate's coming to look at the growing piece of land four times seems surprising. In the Western tradition we have been so accustomed to have things happen in sets of three, but four – as four directions – is significant in an Indian context.

Myths communicate their hidden knowledge by appealing in part to the unconscious as well as the cerebral side of our personalities. Myths repeated often enough have the ability to establish our identity, to mold personality, and to generate commitment.

Abstraction and Intellectual Questioning

These three stories make use of concrete images such as rivers, ropes, rafts, animals, and mountains. However, they are not imaginative stories. That is to say, they do not build on the free association of disparate images.

This is one of the areas where a structural analysis is weak. Structuralism bases its discussion upon the relation it finds between images in a story without taking into account the understanding that was in the minds of the original narrators. Without this understanding new meanings are often simply inserted into the images by the modern critic. This occasions what can be called the perceptive fallacy where meanings, which are not drawn from the myth itself, are imposed upon the text or ceremony. A successful analysis of myth is not possible without reference to the religious institutions that generated the myth in the first place.

What is ultimately communicated in myth is quite non-imaginative and highly abstract. Consider the passage "In the beginning there was no sun, no moon, and no stars. All was dark, and everywhere there was only water." Although the statement is straightforward, the conception that lies behind it is hardly simple. Origin myths in which sun, moon, stars or anything else have no existence are never easy to comprehend. Non-existence and nothingness are puzzling ideas.

Those who conceived such myths had to be highly abstract thinkers. And if their myths would have impact there had to be some minimal familiarity with abstract ideas among their audience as well!

Water only! If the image, 'everywhere there was only water,' is taken seriously, we are describing a world lacking the categories of space and time. It is impossible to sustain such notions on the level of imagination, and yet this is precisely what a myth calls upon its hearers to do. The role of myth is to pique curiosity, hint at the unexpected, and so, using imagery outside the image, to lead us to insight.

Although myths constantly raise issues that are at root philosophical or theological, myths and mythmakers do not proceed to solve them — at least not philosophically. For example the Maidu story, in characteristic fashion, does not linger in the world of abstract speculation about water. It moves on to concrete images. A raft suddenly appears coming from the north containing two solid individuals. Their appearance in the story and the specific action they undertake comes as a great relief.

While myths do not give didactic answers to the problems they raise, we cannot do without them. They give us a needed glimpse of the world behind ordinary reality by breaking through the world of everyday experience.

Similarity of Dynamic and Disagreement of Results

Myths work from a common dynamic but even when they are addressing the same question they do not have the same tale to tell. The Maidu, Genesis and Arrernte myths all set out to tell about the initial formation of the cosmos, but they do not give the same answer.

The Maidu myth follows a form common among North American Indians.[25] It sees the origins of the world as flowing from the combined activity of several coordinate forces. One of them is the ancestral figure Earth-Initiate who comes from above. Those in the boat, whatever they may be, do not come from there. The story then goes on to describe two ancestral figures, Earth-Initiate and Turtle, who will play active roles in constructing the earth in more detail. However, these two can act only in the presence of a third the Father-of-the-Secret-Society, whose role is obscure at this stage of the story. Even these three figures must look outside themselves to find a bit of soil that they need before they can perform any action in the world. The major point of the Maidu story is that many forces must concur if the world is to come into being.

The description of Earth-Initiate might lead the unwary to think of him as the senior partner on the raft, and that the multiplication of the earth can be regarded as his sole responsibility. Nonetheless he requires the active support of others. Turtle must dive for soil since without it there would be nothing to multiply and expand.[26]

While the story of origins in the Maidu myth makes clear that several actors are required, it avoids any form of dualism.

Dualism posits two independent principals such as might be found in Taoism or in an extreme form among Manicheans. Turtle and Earth-Initiate are occupants of the raft and neither is presented in the story as a superior or a shadow principle of the other.

The Genesis story like the Maidu story also begins in uncharted waters, but in Genesis the origins of all activity pivots around the work of Elohim. Elohim is, of course, a plural Semitic form meaning 'the gods'. But the action described in the myth does not refer to a plurality. It refers to the work of a single actor who produces everything that comes to be. The form of the story as we now have it shows the primordial water and land as passive. Neither are presented to God or are they needed by God in any way. Nor do the various creatures of the world look back to multiple principles for their origin. The notion that God is the source of all becomes even more striking when the Genesis story is read against the backdrop of the preceding Sumerian myths where the gods are shown subduing and conquering the ancestral forces that have preceded them.[27]

The Genesis account of creation is considerably simpler than the Maidu account, at least in its main story line. There is only one major figure in Genesis, instead of the concert of two or three that occur in the Maidu story. In Genesis Elohim alone acts, and from his activity we have everything that we now see. There is neither support nor opposition for the Divine activity. When God rests on the seventh day all activity of a creative variety also ceases conclusively.

The Genesis and the Maidu myths of origin do not exhaust the possibilities of explaining how the cosmos came to be. The ancestral Dreaming figure of the Arrernte myth the Nambakula does not require any subordinate principle when shaping a particular landscape. The Nambakula is the unique active

31

principle, but he is not the sole actor in the Dreaming period. In the Dreaming the transformation of the land is a work complemented by other Dreaming ancestors. Nor should it be forgotten that prior to all the Dreaming ancestors the land was there brooding and waiting for the activation that will transform it from, we could say, an un-manifest to a manifest state. Aboriginal stories of origin stress the importance of the land, the constructive work of multiple Dreaming ancestors in forming and shaping it, and their continued presence on it, in the normal time of the post-Dreaming.

CHAPTER IV

THE WORK OF MYTHS

Myths offer a wealth of poetic imagery in telling their tales. Their almost scatter-gun approach has something to capture every imagination, but underneath their imagery lies a central statement. These stories are not loose and muddled bits of narrative that can be manipulated in one direction or the other to suit an individual taste or the needs of a particular society. Rather myth is an essential element that permits individuals to digest the welter of facts and experiences of daily living.

The Mythic Process

Each of the narratives discussed, Genesis, the Maidu and the Arrernte accounts, gives a very definite answer to fundamental questions about the origin of the universe. Divine beings may be eternal but was something else eternal as well? Is the initial formation of the world the work of a solitary actor or several? Do primordial principles require a pre-existing element to help them in their work? Is their activity the work of many, acting in concert or in a tension with each other? While the narrative elements of myths may overlap and though we may find convergence in the various visions of the unseen reality that they describe, in their core teachings the individual myths remain separated.

Origin narratives, the type of story we have been dealing with, form only one part, usually the opening part, of a much longer story sequence. Although they tell of the earliest events origin stories need not have been composed first. Genesis is recognized, for example, as a late book in the Bible probably not set down in its present form until the Exile.

Not surprisingly origin stories pick up traditions about the positioning of humanity in the cosmos, the terms of human work and leisure, human brokenness, the relations between the sexes, sin, and death; traditions which are given in more detail elsewhere in the cycle. While all religions say something about these themes they do not place the same emphasis on each of them. Religions are not, after all, saying the same thing.[28]

Over the years myths can dress themselves anew, but they do not lose sight of their main purpose. Their core teachings are enduring and resilient. The colonial experience of the twentieth century has taught us that religious myths can continue to inculcate their vision even in the face of determined cultural competition.

The divergence of meaning inherent in myths belies the oversimplification that all religions are at root saying the same thing. The origin stories in all religions do not come down to a single meaning. They are, in fact, a poetic way of expressing views that cannot be expressed readily or as forcefully in any other way. As we learn to appreciate the values inherent in religious myths we will not find that "hero with a thousand faces," that Joseph Campbell so confidently expected.[29]

How do myths perform their function? It has been suggested by C. G. Jung and others that myths put us in touch with archetypal ideas that have slipped below the level of conscious memory and, when once released, they powerfully influence our moods and actions.[30] Myths, they say, will express universal values based on the universality of human thought processes. But the teaching of myths is not always so immediately transparent even to psychiatry. After all, concealment is a part of a myth's charm. A major burden of an interpreter of religious myths is to winnow out that essential core from the flowering and meandering imagery of the narrative. No little part of an interpreter's skill is the ability to find the level at which the seemingly random fragments of a story fit together to reinforce the central teaching of the story line.

It is not necessary for us to enter the ongoing discussion of whether individuals are 'wired' by the long process of evolution to respond to archetypal patterns or whether these patterns are interiorized during the normal socialization processes in childhood. Furthermore, whether some of them are so universal that they will always appear in every culture, or whether they are simply the patterns of local behavior in a particular community is another point that we need not deal with here. It will be enough for our purposes to note that some elements in the subconscious, which we will call archetypal, have a major role to play in providing stable patterns for human consciousness.

Whatever explanation is adopted for archetypes it is clear that myths organize the human personality in its response to the mysteries of human existence and the universe. It is the function of myth to draw our attention to the mystery that lies below the surface of consciousness. They are also charged with the task of enabling the individual and the community to cope with mystery.

Evaluation of Myths

When dealing with religious myth it is first necessary to listen and then to get the story straight. The fact that myths make different statements about reality leads us to draw an important corollary — it is unwise to think of myths simply as projections of the patterns to be found in the consciousness of humanity.

Fortunately for an interpreter the task is made easier because myths are not found in splendid isolation. Individual stories are part of a myth cycle that allows them to continually interact with one another.

In religions depending on oral traditions the stories of the gods and other tales with mythic elements are told and retold — acted and reenacted. Whatever the burden a particular story has, there will be numerous occasions where it must interact with other myths to clarify and hone its message.

In religions with written traditions, religions of the book, there are community editors who have acquired authority, either by their position or by popularity, who sort out matters. It is their task to accept, reject, adapt, and to even hold variant accounts together in tension to refine the various meanings implicit in the stories. But even with written traditions the oral telling is still a powerful force. Literate societies retain a good deal of dependence on oral presentations. The written word, after all, is a relatively recent development in the history of the human race. Even prolific readers are just as likely to come across myths and rituals in sermons or on television as they are to read about them.

It has been said, half-humorously, that under such conditions no myth has ever been told in the same way twice since the creativity of the presenter always intervenes. There is truth in this, but the retellings of a myth present a pattern that is ultimately consistent with its key teaching. And no less importantly, the retellings present a pattern consistent with the larger cycle of a community's religious myths.

The retelling also explains how myths can offer many messages. Retelling stories in varying forms encourages a search for the deeper inner symbolism. Listeners ruminating over the changing signs and images will be encouraged to look for a central core of meaning.

In trying to get the story straight it would be a mistake to assume that every element, every action and image can be read off like a recipe, like sign posts by the roadside. Myths do not express themselves in transparent terms but through imagery, and often changing imagery at that. This fact points to an important truth, myths are driven by symbols rather than by signs. I will have more to say about symbolism later but it will be enough to note here that symbolism is not identical with signifying. Signs have a one-to-one relation with their object. Like signs in an airport they can be read in a literal fashion. Symbols are intended to be opaque. They must speak indirectly because symbols engage us with mysteries that can never be clearly known.

Myths make use of signs however. This is the reason the cast of characters of a myth narrative may change with the years, and change from one geographical location to another. New material may be woven into an account or dropped out again as fashions change or in response to the feelings of the audience. A traumatic event, like the coming of the white man, may be introduced into a myth cycle. Story segments can be borrowed from one religion and be reprocessed to do duty in service of another.

As already noted alternate forms of the Maidu myth of origin, for example, have been recognized in many parts of North America and elsewhere.[31] Turtle is routinely replaced by other animals, like the loon or beaver, which are sent to recover earth hidden in a lake or marsh. The time required to bring the earth or mud back may also vary from years to a few days. Signs sometimes serve as markers pointing to other myths. The number of days, or moons, or seasons required to acquire the soil usually play a role in subsequent stories of the same myth cycle. Underneath the signs that change, there lies a basic teaching. Some other creature can easily take over the work of Turtle. Turtle may be away a few days or six years, but he must return with soil if the myth is to be complete. The point is there must always be someone else and Earth-Initiate cannot act alone.

Similarly, in the Dreaming stories of the Australian Aborigines the land can be peopled by all sorts of ancestral beings — no one of them common to all the tribes — but every Dreaming landscape must have at least some of them. The purpose of the ancestor remains the same - to shape and allot the land. The purpose is displayed in different ways at different times and in different places because land, unlike purpose, is not abstract but a particular thing.

Signs may change but the core meaning does not change easily. This is the key to the puzzle of why a myth can be traced back hundreds even thousands of years when a community may not remember details beyond two or three generations. Myths are durable not because of local imagery — they can withstand all sorts of casual modifications - but because what they symbolize remains constant.

Myths and Philosophy

Myths are not designed to offer proof, or to be a kind of philosophy for the non-philosophic of mind. We must not forget that faith and acceptance is required if a myth is to have transforming power.

In the nineteenth century it was popular to explain myths as the rustic science of primitive peoples. Such theories are deservedly out of fashion now. Bronislaw Malinowski argued against such views that were put forward by James Frazer and others.[32] From his own experience he had come to realize that traditional cultures were quite capable of solving their problems scientifically. What is even more relevant Malinowski saw that they were well able to distinguish scientific from non-scientific behavior. The Islanders he stayed with had systematic ways of getting workable answers for their practical problems. Gardeners in tribal villages had learned to manage their plots with exacting care and skill. No fishing party would start out without considering the time of day, the weather, the state of the creeks, and the best bait or snare to use. When it is time to build a canoe, wood would be cut in the proper shape from a suitable sort of tree. When a new tool or a new type of timber was introduced improvements were made by replacing customary designs. Stone axes gave way to steel ax heads without posing any difficulties for the myths told about them.

The nineteenth century attempts to interpret myths as primitive science introduced a host of inappropriate questions and false problems. Myths do not give scientific accounts of the topics they deal with. Nor do they give historical accounts either. Their concern is not so much with actual causes as with presenting an order of reality that makes sense in terms of a community's overall understanding of the universe.

Concern for logical, scientific or even historical neatness must not be allowed to interfere with the reading of a myth, insofar as it is a myth. Making 'scientific sense' or 'historical sense' may distract from picking out the truth that the myth articulates.

Not everything necessary will be addressed in any single myth, but the full cycle of myths can be expected to deal with most human needs. Myths offer consolation, encourage brave deeds, or counsel resignation, suggest a goal for life, gods' plan for people — and so make their worth felt.

A myth cycle simultaneously has a mundane and otherworldly content. It is pregnant with meaning at several levels. It reflects the sacred traditions of the people and expresses the wisdom of their literature, oral traditions, and religious rituals.

Once a community accepts a myth cycle the psyches of individuals become organized around its central teachings. They are an important force in the socializing of individuals, and also serve to organize the fabric of society.

Since myths make a statement that is largely symbolic, and not scientific, they must be repeated and remembered lest their affect upon the conscious psyche be lost. Since the understanding that myths present are of something we cannot know by normal means, the correct meaning of a myth is always at risk. The easy road to rationalizing or historicizing always lies open! Attempts made to reduce the tension inherent in a myth by either explaining away the mystery behind it, or by treating the story as a relic of a quaint antiquarian past will miss the point. If they are to retain their impact it is necessary to get the story 'straight'. Myths are stories endowed with authority. They organize experience in ways in which experience does not have to be organized! Myths require continual interaction and remembrance if they are to remain relevant to those who hear them.

Values Latent in Myth

What can we say of myths that have been drawn from one context into another? How do the teachings that the myths put forward in one context change in their new home? Are the new devotions drawn into the context of the past and so become one with them? Or does what is present in the new symbolism impose itself on the old religion, effectively eclipsing the old? Should we say that a new range of imagery now reveals the latent possibilities of the old myths? These questions touch on enculturation — the way that religious truths are grafted into another story — that is beyond the scope of the present inquiry.

Mythic symbolism should not be regarded as something forever static and fixed, as if it was a variant of a Platonic form. However, the cycles of stories presented in a religious community have a unity of their own. We can expect that attitudes that are essentially incompatible with central symbols will be received briefly but will be weeded out over time.

Myths talk confidently about the purposes of gods, while all the time protesting that no one has been god's councilor. Myths encapsulate the religious experience of a people and so provide a context for interpreting the whole of life. They become a part of the common store of a people's knowledge so that without them a community cannot long survive, at least not as the community it once was.

Myths have objective value and they impart a content, albeit in a non-didactic form. What they have to say is public knowledge, that is, knowledge that is interpersonal and communicable. The Australian Aborigines understood this and made sure their Dreaming stories were repeated in conversation and ritual to each successive generation.

Myths have a peculiar power to communicate and impress themselves on persons because they appeal to the emotions as well as to the mind and imagination. They continually attract attention because they always seem to convey more than a rational analysis would extract. Myths conceal as well as reveal their object. The stories may be opaque but with patience they will always teach us more than meets the eye.

Other Concerns of Myth Cycles

In addition to origin stories myth cycles have stories that orient a community to the world. H. Storm an American Indian expressed this well:

Whenever we hear a story, it is as if we were physically walking down a particular path that has been created for us. Everything we perceive upon this path or around it becomes part of our experience, both individually and collectively.[33]

The Aborigines of Australia insist that in stories of the Dreaming it is land in all its aspects and through all seasons that becomes a focus of their psyche. So much so that rather than possessing the land the land now possesses them. Myth cycles often tell about the calling together of a particular people, their goals and destiny, and the role they are fated to play in the world.

Not surprisingly worry and hope about death orients humanity in the cosmos. 'Why death' is a universal question without a universal answer. Why are humans ordained to die? Why should death have come into the world? Who can escape it? Who can assist in the encounter with it? If God is good, and creation is good, why has evil and death entered the world. In mythical accounts death is assigned to various causes. In Genesis it is accredited to human disobedience. In Sumerian accounts it is a result of the jealousy of the gods. In North American cycles it is a fortuitous mistake and in Oceanic cycles it is simply a natural necessity.

Myth cycles deal with mundane but nonetheless important issues for which rational analysis has no fixed answer. Questions such as how should illness and aging be borne? what are the proper relations between the sexes? what is suitable public behavior? what is proper relationship between husband and wife? what personal responsibility do we have for our actions before the divine? These are all subject matter for mythology.

Chapter V

MYTH AND HISTORY

Let us now consider myths as they give a true understanding of the past. It is apparent that myths can not be relied upon directly for specific information about tribal histories or other ancient memories of the race. How then do myths contribute to our knowledge of the past?

First, history employs myths to illustrate particular events, and sometimes uses myths to describe a sequence of events. The Olympic Games at Sydney provide an example of the latter use of myth in history. In the opening ceremonies a series of images were shown — stockmen, icons of the Bush; an Aboriginal Elder guiding a young girl; the building of the Sydney Harbor Bridge; the coming of the post war immigrants; and much more. The sequence presented the history of the growth of Australia into a multicultural society.

Secondly, fragments of myth are embedded in the local history of many communities. A good example of this type of historical use of myth is in the legends that 'George Washington slept here.' On the United States East Coast many towns can point to a house where he slept.

Furthermore the significance of space, time, and causality of historical events can depend on mythic connections. An example of this would be the wide-open spaces of a western prairie farm in the United States.

This question of the relation of history and myth falls naturally into two parts. The first will see how much human history there is in myth. The second part will show how much myth dominates our histories.

Since it is a fact that myths attract us to the world of nature, we will deal first with myth as nature symbolism. This will lead to an examination of nature symbolism as it affects ideas of place and time in human history. Next we will see how myths escape from being mere nature symbolism and open up deeper understandings about the true meaning of human life. The second part of the question will, as we have said, deal with how history is driven by mythical values.

Religious and secular myths share certain features. They both affect the conscious and unconscious parts of personality, and they both require a 'leap of faith' – acceptance of things not based on factual information. However, it should be kept in mind what is distinctive about each of them.

Myth as an expression of Nature Symbolism

The content of myth can be secular or religious. Secular myths rearrange well-known material in order to make a point about the culture or history of a people. The result is not history and should not be accepted as such. Religious myths, on the other hand, make room for history in order to tell about the origin and causes of events that could not be known by ordinary means.

Religious myths are stories about the gods or about the mysteries of the universe that are in some way beyond our ken. These stories, which seem simple enough at first hearing, cannot really be understood if taken literally. When myths speak about the gods, or of the mysterious dealings of the gods with humanity, fundamentalists need not apply! Saint John's Gospel tells us, "No one has ever seen God."[34] On this point virtually all scholars and philosophers agree with him. If we want to speak about God, or the gods, or of our relationship to God — if we suppose a relationship exists, between God and ourselves — we have to resort to special language. We must have recourse to stories that speak in symbolic terms.

In general terms, symbolizing can be described as the substitution of one image for another in the service of greater knowledge. Later I will discuss the nature, origins and noetic of symbolism. For the present it is enough to note that symbols are based on imagery. The images are simple enough to recognize, but they refer beyond themselves and suggest other meanings that are much more difficult to comprehend.

Nature symbolism is brought to our attention in many ways. At times it is taken from childhood stories, such as: the sea where an eternally feminine mermaid lives; or of a Milky Way where each star represents an ancestor; or of dealings with animals, like the Old Man Coyote, who in a human voice gives wise or deceptive advice. Sometimes symbolism is taken second hand from indigenous peoples. When we recall the symbolism of indigenous people, we are often impressed by their careful use of nature. In their stories the lives of human beings are a world of hunting and of gathering, or maybe of farming, but with scant reference to cities, trade or commerce. As a rule symbolism with a religious flavor turns to the imagery drawn from the natural world and the broader cosmos.

There is an extensive scholarly literature exploring the interpretation of natural symbolism. Mircea Eliade has established the parameters of the modern discussion.[35] Sam Gill gives a guide to interpreting life by appropriating the nature symbolism of Native American Peoples.[36] James Cowan gives a fanciful remembrance of Australian Aboriginal material.[37] Mary Douglas tells, from an academic point of view, the story of what natural symbolism accomplishes.[38] The reason for the popularity of nature symbolism is its easy accessibility while the extensive scholarly interest is due to its claims of universality.

Concrete phenomena, such as the returning warmth of the sun in the spring, are easily recognized as a cause for the rapid growth of existing trees and plants, and as responsible for the budding of new life. Even in cities, away from the countryside, the sun's heat seems to be a contributing cause of the increase in all kinds of human and animal activity. In spring, with the return of the sun's light, optimism is in the air. It is a time for acquiring food after a long winter of hibernation, a time to take chances, a time for engaging in the pursuit of love or money. The sun becomes a sign signaling the return of life and the nurturing of all human possibilities. It is an easy step to conceive of the solar disc as the unique source for the collective good things of the earth. From being an impersonal force energizing the whole physical world the sun can be personified as a beneficent being with a mind and personality of its own. It develops from being a sign to being a symbol of universal good. Scholars tell us that throughout the ages the sun has been an important factor in the religious stories of virtually all people.

Stories of other concrete realities in nature like the moon, the oceans, fire, specific animals and birds, such as the bear and the eagle, are spread broadly across cultures and centuries. The symbols presented in myths associated with these natural phenomena have such a wide range of acceptance that we can speak of their cosmic and universal value.

Sacred Space and Sacred Time

In his widely read book, *The Sacred and the Profane*, the late Mircea Eliade has performed a service in popularizing two notions that go hand in hand with nature symbolism — place and time. He distinguishes between ordinary, that is secular space, and what he calls sacred space.

Ordinary space can be characterized as homogeneous throughout. A journey through ordinary space could be a drive through miles and miles of the gray undistinguished and impersonal blocks of the faceless suburbs at the outskirts of a typical Northern European or American city. In such space one shopping center looks much like any other so that shoppers can become disoriented and wonder where they are. In such a space a lack of something to do is not an invitation to leisure, but to desperation.

Sacred space is unlike the secularized space that dominates much of a modern landscape. Sacred space is permeated by the power of the gods. It is a space oriented toward a goal. In such a space there are fixed points that break up the homogeneity because they have a story to tell about the gods. These fixed points are sacred places. Paradoxically sacred space is organized so that a humane way of living is possible.

If we look at the landscape through the eyes of indigenous persons, such as the aboriginal Australians for example, we find sites with differing levels of sacredness. Women cannot visit some locations. Others cannot be visited by uninitiated men, although they are open to all the initiates. Some locations are fully open only to ritual specialists, as A. P. Elkin called them, the 'men of high degree'.[39] These places are separated since they are associated with power. Under certain conditions they can be open to the inruption of powerful forces that, for want of a better description, can be called more than ordinary powers. A sacred landscape is pocketed with areas having such special value. It is there that the gods can appear.

Living in a sacred space entails a shift from living in chaos to being in a cosmos. Before the Enlightenment the medieval community of Europe lived in its cosmos where the world of nature was treated as a book of symbols with the name of God written on every page. Living in a cosmos also involved living in a world of sacred time – a time apart from ordinary time.[40]

Ordinary time, that is the scientifically measured clockwork time of our day, proceeds moment-by-moment. The clock was a momentous breakthrough at the beginning of the modern age. It brought the ability to measure and express time in numerical form and made experimental science possible. The proliferation of clocks at the end of the fourteenth century, and their perfection in the fifteenth century, was critical for the growth of modern Western life. With the introduction of the clock, moments of time were homogenized and crystallized like units of space. So the procession of events could be disciplined and examined one by one. Time became an onward flow, progressive and without an end in view. Extending indefinitely across homogeneous space, time became linear. In linear time one event follows the other without interruption, and more importantly without emphasis and without cessation. It was the formula for organizing production. But it was also a formula that makes human existence boring and monotonous. It introduced the chaos of the workaholic!

Sacred time, like sacred space, is very different from linear time. Sacred time is concerned with moments that are not like other moments. Sacred time is not linear, but circular and reversible. It can turn back upon itself and review a past event as if it were in the present. Sacred time is found in the language of the myths. Sacred time concerned itself with the special moments during which the gods entered into the cosmos — when they acted upon the world. In the world of sacred time it is always possible to return again to origins. In the world of myth the action of the gods is permanent — enduring. All that is necessary is to call it into the present once more.

Myths about the time of origins always held a special place in primal religions. The time of origins called the human community back to important events when the gods showed forth their greatest power. They recall us to the time of the formation of the world that is the model for future worlds. Mircea Eliade developed the idea that in primal religions myths of origin routinely called adherents to return to their time of origins. It was a way of avoiding the terror of linear history — of avoiding existence as meaningless. Sacred time points toward a cosmos where all is ordered, unsullied, and in perfect balance. This attitude is itself a myth, of course, and a most powerful one — the myth of the eternal return.[41] It fits in well with the theory developed by Carl Jung and his followers that the hero needs to return in the second half of his life to the roots that gave him birth.

If this recall to the time of the formation of the world was universal, then, this myth of eternal return was a cosmic myth, and so not without its dangers. It could be regarded simply as the reflection of the human community on the ordered movements of visible universe — the sense of a return generated by observing the perpetual rising and setting of the sun, the regularity of the monthly waxing and waning of the moon, the ordered round of the seasons, the cycle of birth and reawakening in plant life in spring. These observations are older than Babylon. These observations had produced the celestial idolatry of ancient paganism, the gods of the rising and dying annual vegetation cycle.

Symbolism in Religions of the Book

Despite the universality and attractiveness of nature symbolism it has always been met in revealed religions with a certain amount of caution, if not outright trepidation. The very universality of this symbolism was a cause of worry. It is often referred to, somewhat pejoratively, as mere cosmic symbolism. The symbolism derived from nature is universal, but in the end it consists of merely human observations about the universe. It is a symbolism that reflects gods made with human hands — or perhaps it should be said gods made in the human mind. Revealed religion, religions of the Book, feared that too much reliance on the world of nature symbolism would reduce religion back to its naturalistic and pagan roots. Nature mythology might be well and good for ancient primal religions, but revealed religions handled things differently.

Judaism and its daughter Christianity knew all about sacred time, but not in the same way as nature religions. Human beings organize all experience in terms of space and time. But for revealed religions there was no reason for supposing that they must find the gods in special sacred places and that they must always return to local spots to find them. Judaism and Christianity found the acts of God to be present in a historical sequence.[42] Time in both the Old and New Testaments was not circular, not a return, but linear and progressive.

The story of the Jews is above all to be found in Exodus, an escape story. The escape from Egypt, the wandering through the Sinai desert during a period of forty years, and the encounter with God in the Sinai was a defining experience for the Jewish people. However, the Jews did not return to Egypt or the Sinai, but looked forward to entering a new and Promised Land.

Around this central story of escape, wandering, and finding God, other events of the Bible are arranged in a linear way. The history recounts the essential events including: the deeds of the ancient patriarchs, Abraham, Isaac and Jacob; the descent into Egypt from Canaan; the story central to Judaism, the Exodus to Mount Sinai under Moses; the entrance to the Promised Land; the Kingdom of David in the Promised Land; the Exile in Babylon, predicted by the Prophets; the return from Exile to Jerusalem; the rebuilding of the Temple during the Commonwealth; the revolts of the Machabees. All these events were presented in temporal fashion looking forward to the advent of the Messiah in a time to come.

In the New Testament the advent of Christ was both a fulfillment and the continuation of the story. The destruction of the Temple in AD 70 and the ruinous war in AD 135 simply underscored, for Christians at any rate, that the people's fulfillment lay in the future. There was not to be a cyclical return to Temple roots, precious as they were.

The experience of God by the Jewish and Christian people encouraged them to develop an ongoing and deepening understanding of God's dealings with humanity. God did not show his greatest power at the beginning, but rather throughout time![43]

Escape from the World of Nature

The first eleven chapters of Genesis contain stories that give every appearance of falling into the category of cosmic symbolism. However, they are not simply general observations about the world of nature. Cosmic myths draw their wisdom from the universal observations of nature by humans. But the human interpretation of this experience is by no means universal. The stories of Genesis offer more specific messages than just a general observation of nature.

The Garden of Eden is described as a place of idyllic human existence, something that, in fact, is contrary to the universal experience of nature. The tree of knowledge in the garden is a temptation to evil. The donning of clothes by Adam and Eve is the sign that the original innocence of the universe has been shattered and the relations between humanity and its author have soured. Adam and Eve are expelled from the garden and sent out to labor and deal with the struggle for life. The story goes on to set out the parameters on which human life will be lived — 'you will work for your bread; you will find joy, but suffering in childbirth.' The subtle differences in the Genesis stories from other myths of origin become clearer when they are compared with the other origin myths to be found in the ancient Near East.

At this point, it would be well to also ask whether the myths of primal religions are, as is sometimes assumed, completely innocent of history. Stories about the flora and fauna of a neighborhood attract a casual listener, but their total effect cannot be reduced to observations about nature.

The impulse to equate winding, twisting watercourses, so characteristic of streams of Australia's Northern Territory, with the work of a huge snake scurrying along the landscape on its way to the sea comes readily to mind. The metaphor of a river as a snake is obvious and unsophisticated. It is the sort of imagery that suggests to anyone glancing from the airplane window while flying over the region. The Dreaming ancestor of this region happens to be Kunmanggur the rainbow serpent. But the stories associated with his movements across the landscape cannot be identified with what is seen from the air or on the ground. Each camp where the Dreaming ancestor stopped on his way to the sea, every one of his moves, has a particular story of its own. All the stories gathering from the local communities form a cycle which become an integrated whole. These are stories not concerned solely with cosmic imagery. The story of Kunmanggur the rainbow snake has concrete elements and in that sense makes a historical statement. It is also a story that is not simply cyclical but has trans-natural elements as well.

Myths both Cosmic and Historical

The distinctions between sacred and ordinary space, between linear and circular time, are useful, but they should not be absolutized. There is nothing to prevent cosmic symbolism from being both universal and historical at the same time. Symbols have multiple meanings. In the New Testament the stories of the Kingdom of Heaven as a garden with God as householder thrive on the imagery of the commonplace. But values such as justice, evenhandedness, and peace and tranquility are also proposed in the garden-kingdom image. The imagery of the Kingdom of Heaven is not about a return to the idyllic Garden of Eden, or of a return to any temporal kingdom. The Kingdom of the New Testament is again something unclear and mysterious. It is a divine event, something new, inrushing in Jesus' lifetime.

A careful reader of Israel's sacred texts also recognizes that the images smuggle in many historical references to contemporary Jerusalem, to messianic expectations and to much more. The historical references give the stories a richer and deeper meaning for listeners and they also make them controversial.

Mythical stories can express at the same time both what is natural and what is revealed. Perhaps this is what a Roman

Catholic Deacon in the Australia's Northern Territory had in mind when he wrote, "Before Moses God was with the Aboriginal People." God was not present in his country as someone derived from nature, or from local stories long remembered, but the God present was the God who cared for the followers of Moses and who also cared for them. It is perhaps why another Aboriginal Elder said to me, "Every Dreaming is from the Holy Spirit."

If we are prepared to accept the above statements and agree that the myths of indigenous people have historical elements, that is, aspects that do not come from the observation of nature but are revealed, another question must be raised. Is the context of the religions of Middle East the only appropriate preparation for the Gospel, the only possible praeparatio evangelica? It is a question that I can only touch on here.

Salvation history as it is given in the Scriptures will always have a unique place for the Jewish community since it is the record of that community's life as a people. For the Christian community that history will always be held in high regard since it is the context where the earthly personality of Jesus was formed. On this there can be no hesitation. But is this to deny that the history of every other people is devoid of religious symbolism? It has been suggested that the myths embedded in the history of the Maori people, for example, could be seen as such a history.[44] This implies that something of the personality of God has appeared in that land and that God has intervened in their history too. For Christians who are interested in the possibility of what is termed enculturation, that is seeing the Gospels for what they really are and not in terms of an alien import, the divine presence in the ancient myths provides the groundwork for the Gospels to be at home in every place and culture. Because God has intervened in the history of all peoples, his word could be implanted and find a home there.

Mythic Aspects of History

While all religious myths have some historical references, history for its part has its mythical aspect too. It is an aspect that is generally too much overlooked. Historical discussions in the West since the nineteenth century have the expectation that histories are factual and do not rest on myth. At least, there is an expectation that any mythical stories found are to be exorcised by the historian as thoroughly as possible.

The stance that history is purely factual stems from the West's consuming preoccupation with time and, in particular, with time as a progressive experience of event-after-event. From the middle of the nineteenth century scholars entered into the past to find out, as they said, 'what really happened there.'? This view of history was favored by Leopold von Ranke who insisted on historical inquiry based on the study of primary sources. Earlier histories which were inclined to be edifying or propagandist have come to be regarded as biased and old fashioned. His way of conducting research and his manner of writing became models for historians in the nineteenth century.[45] History was to be a study of the past 'warts and all' and without biases or preconceptions. It was the historian's duty to be scientific and look at facts! This was the time when historians began to rummage through state archives and to pour over accounts of court trials and statistical records of all sorts. It was a time for reading the diaries of admirable ancients who had influenced events, and for producing critical editions of important works. Precision in dating past events assumed new significance because if history was linear and developed in linear segments, it had to be fixed to dates that could be agreed upon!

In this climate historians preoccupied themselves with the actions of kings, princes and ecclesiastical elites moving across the stage of political power. Biographies dealt with the men and women who were instrumental in making things happen. Histories tended to personify nations and look at the relationships between nations as actions on a stage. Church histories became the history of Popes, Cardinals, religious leaders, and their relations to the state and to each other.

History all too often was identified with political history. The deficiencies of a history that was nothing more than political events caused attention to shift gradually to social histories of the humbler classes. Histories expanded to include the fate of merchants, weavers, clerks or nuns and the like, caught up in the great events such as the Crusades, the Reformation or the Industrial Revolution. Articles in historical journals offered vignettes that opened small windows on the past. Economic, social and cultural studies were undertaken to round out the understanding of a period, a country or even a religion. Since scholars now knew 'what had really happened,' readers were invited to step outside their own society and become for a brief moment participants of the past.

For Christians there was one moment of history that was privileged and inviting beyond all others — the time of Christ and the days of the very early church. Religious histories were written to help readers to step into what had happened then and see it at first hand, without mythical bias.

It must be confessed, however, that historical analysis of this kind did not always produce an opening to the past. Instead, it often marshaled a vast array of information, factual to a fault, but cut off from its roots and crying out for some principle of organization — an organization that facts alone could not give.

Doubts about the possibility of ever stepping back into a previous time were not long in coming. There was a broad and deep cultural chasm between the experience of reality in the nineteenth and twentieth centuries and the experience of the first or even the thirteenth century. How could a historian be confident of fully entering into the life of another era if parents found the gap between their generation and the next difficult to bridge? How could a gap between twenty or fifty generations be negotiated?

Awareness of the huge gap between present life and life experienced in the past brought a dawning realization that historians were not the neutral bystanders that had been taken for granted. They stood within their own culture that in turn stood on a particular segment of a linear history. Their examination of the past would inevitably be fogged by the presence of their culture with its own particular myths. Unlike the snake, they could not shed their skins. The material collected from the study of historic records now seemed to become doubly opaque — it looked to a past that could never fully be recorded and what was recorded, was seen through the lens of one's own culture. In light of these considerations, history began to lose its vaunted objective non-mythical status.

Linear time returns less and less to its origins as it is driven farther and farther away by a steady stream of data generated by new events. Historians and their readers found themselves wrapped up in homogeneous time with its attendant rootlessness and disorientation. It is an experience so well described in a famous phrase written at the beginning of the modern age:

> Tomorrow, and tomorrow, and tomorrow creeps
> in this petty pace from day to day to the last syllable
> of recorded time ... all is sound and fury, signifying
> nothing.[46]

In the grip of unadulterated linear time chaos begins again. Even history, it seemed, required myths after all!

Progress and Linear Time

In the world of linear history one myth has surfaced that has served to keep the terror of chaos at bay and even generate optimism. If events paced one after another in a sequential line were to mean something there needs to be some goal or end. To save itself linear history generated a myth of eternal non-return — the myth of progress. It became common for historians to speak of growth and development. The notion that human history was a pageant of progress, an ever expanding and more perfect development, is, of course, a myth. Like any myth it tries to tell us what we cannot know by ordinary means. It interprets experience in ways that it does not have to be interpreted.

Like other myths, progress was beyond judgment. As a principle for organizing events progress was a premise to be accepted and not proven. Looking back over human records with the searchlight of progress in hand historians began to discern an outline of the growth and development in human affairs. Life began simply enough in the human community with hunter-gatherers, then it centered on herdsmen and small farmers, this passed to village life, and on to the town and metropolis. All this was accompanied by gains in art, culture, science and technologies made possible by a complex and developing society. As the myth of progress required, life looked forward to even a brighter future.

Religions, it was thought, would have made progress too. Religious sensibility began with an attachment to the forces of nature and moved forward to an anthropomorphic form of polytheism, then on to the worship of a primary single spiritual being. The worship of the solar disc led upward to a true monotheism found in Judaism — the One who is totally other — and finally to an enlightened form of monotheism in Christianity — the God who entered history.

Whether this is a wholly accurate or a particularly sophisticated account is not a matter of concern here. What is significant is that the values claimed for the myth of progress were routinely positive and optimistic for religion too. The idea of progress implies that the human community in successive ages will continually know more than it did in ages past, that its moral judgments will become even more refined and that the human community will progressively gain control over its destiny.

Like any myth, the myth of progress is self-correcting. It did not matter if historical studies, by almost any index chosen, showed that human progress had not been continuous or evenly spread over the centuries. It did not matter if progress had not been shared equally by all societies and cultures. It did not matter if progress in gentility, honesty, and sensitivity to religious values failed to match the increases in material wealth. The myth of development seemed unassailable. The vanguard of progress lay firmly in Europe, the Americas and their satellites and would develop from there. Progress said that development was destined to become universal and ultimately be the patrimony of all people. Progress assures us that all humanity is moving forward to ever more enlightened times.

The assurance that the myth of progress inspired drew the sting out of the rootlessness inherent in linear time. History now had its myth.

The Engine of History

But if progress is merely a myth why should anyone adopt it? Why should anyone baldly assume that human life proceeds in a developmental way? What is the engine of progress? Several reasons have been offered.

For Georg Hegel, the German nineteenth century idealist philosopher, the engine driving human progress was the work of mind.[47] In a dialogic way mind actively mulled over the prospects and possibilities inherent in a given situation and saw roads of development which had not been apparent before. Such opportunities that were uncovered and then grasped created progress. Our present human conditions provided a platform upon which the next stage of growth will be built. Hegel's careful description of the shape of the inevitable intellectual development of the human community was worked out in painstaking detail in The Phenomenology of Spirit. It is a book which enthralled, and still enthralls many through the philosophers and historians who have absorbed its point of view. Hegel argued that the real was the rational and that the rational was the real. This reality was developmental and moved through human history by a dialectical process of thesis (initial position) through its opposition, the antithesis, where the ensuing conflict brought forward a synthesis, itself to be annulled by a further antithesis. This dialectic was continuous, evolutionary and progressive. Despite its brilliance, however, an ungrounded hopefulness about the correctness and the goodness of human choices cling to the Hegelian doctrine.

In the hands of Karl Marx, the economist, philosopher, and revolutionist the engine of progress was not in the mind, but elsewhere.[48] The Hegelian notion of a dialectical process of development was retained, but economic forces, and not mind, was what drove the process. In the long run it was the economic forces, which at once spurred production and engendered competition between classes that assured continued orderly, reasoned, growth and development. In the Marxist system the myth of progress remained, but now under new management.

In religious hands the engine of progress, as we might expect, assumed religious forms. In the West the engine of human progress was found in the gradual working out of a divine plan, the history of salvation.[49] Human activity motivated by religious concerns was the locus for God's continuous intervention into history. As a consequence, humanity could look back over the centuries with awe and some amount of pride about what had been accomplished. More significantly, the faithful could look forward in confidence to further progress in the future as the divine plan took deeper hold.

Some religionists in harmony with the legacy of Hegelian theory argued that a process involving a dialogue with the gospel drove religion. A few went so far as to say that the dialogue was between humanity and god. God was a god of history who interacted with the world of events, not a fixed abstraction. Divinity itself was in process, since God too had stepped within linear time. The myth of progress spawned a further myth, the myth of a humanized divinity. Human activity became the place where the god(s) were found. The philosopher Max Scheler saw humanity as called to co-struggle in alliance with the divinity.[50] Even more influential were the process theories of Alfred North Whitehead and his disciple Charles Hartshorne.[51]

The proposition that human history is the place where gods are found is quite different from the proposition that humanity is the place where divinity creates itself. When human activity becomes the place where divinity happens it is not the gods who are exercising creative power, it is human beings. The gods become a convenient cloak to cover a human form.

For Christians the Incarnation of Christ is the preeminent revelation of God in history. The life of the church is said to be the continuation of that Incarnation, but not in the sense that Christ is to be found in human activities. The idea that God is to be found in human activity is quite different from the idea that God inrupted into human history. When the gods inrupted into history they did so to transform it, to renew it, and to give it direction. The moment when they enter is not simply a point in linear time. Rather, it becomes once again a time of origin. The Incarnation was such a point in time. It occurred as a linear point that can be dated and is an event that transformed the world. In this sense it is a point of origin that Christians can interiorize through meditation and ritual in order to be recaptured by its power. It could be said that the historical events of the New Testament have become for Christians a moment of their eternal Dreaming.

In recent generations the myth of progress and the idea that human history is a process where divinity occurs is difficult to sustain. This century has seen the horrors of two major wars and a host of minor ones. The ghosts of the holocaust and of a nuclear attack have not been laid to rest. Fear and terror have returned to the streets of modern cities. Although there is a heightened consciousness of injustice that has not yet brought about its elimination! Not surprisingly, the myth of progress in linear time has begun to unravel.

Popular movements everywhere are struggling to draw away from grand empires making universal claims. Carving out local arrangements of their own designs is in favor. The searches for identity, for delving into one's ethnicity, for racial pride, for resurgent nationalism, and for sectarian fundamentalism are responses to be expected. Significantly these popular movements are looking outside linear time. They are looking for roots. These roots can be in the depth of the unconscious, in human nature, or in extraterrestrial revelations, but not in a progressive future.

With the erosion of the myth of progress the reproach associated with linear time has been revived. There is a deep sense of chaos and formlessness in society, and of violence. The questions being asked: — who am I? what is my identity? what is the proper place of my nation in the sun? — These are not questions about the future, but are concerns about the present. Nor are they the type of question that will be answered by gathering more information, by surveys, opinion polls, or by undertaking new experiences. What is needed is the re-enchantment of the world — to meet the gods at the beginning of time when they showed forth their greatest power.

History does have mythic values, but they may not be grounded in linear history. More likely they will be discovered in signs and symbols that look through and beyond linear progress to other ways of assigning human values.

For Christians, origins will be found in the Scriptures and the ongoing in the life of the church as it returns to its origins through stories and ritual. These stories and ritual refer to vital historical events of the first century and have the status of myth in that they eternally reorganize human life according to God's plan. God's plan, more mysterious than progress in linear time, is for human beings to be remade in the image and likeness of God. To the eternal original of our likeness we must return.

For Christians and non-Christians disenchantment with progress generates a need for symbolism to provide a meaning to life. They will search for these symbols since symbols must be found and cannot be manufactured. No community can live for long in the formless world of ordinary space and time.

CHAPTER VI

MYTH AND RITUAL

In examining the relationship between myth and ritual it will be discovered that they are bound tightly together. This is particularly evident in religious rituals where myths about the gods are acted out. Academic discussions have raged without a well-defined purpose whether myth has priority over ritual, or ritual has priority over myth.[52]

What is clear is that ritual has a distinctive role to play in mythology, a role that is powerful and not well understood. W. R. Smith launched a school of thought called the myth-ritual school.[53] It emphasized the importance of ritual acts in religion. Later this school of thought stressed the (annual) ritual surrounding divine kingship, which they considered to be universal in the ancient world. Based on this thinking, some scholars proposed myth to be a virtual libretto that accompanied all ritual acts. These ideas had to be eventually abandoned. However, an opposing concept that holds that primitive ritual has no intelligible meaning should be equally rejected as extreme. The truth is that rituals are performed because they are embedded in a context of meaning. Although words may not be expressed in the course of the ritual a story line will always be in the background.

Orientation to a Transcendent power

Ritual requires measured sequence and repetition. Unlike myths, rituals are essentially embedded in time, though not necessarily in linear time. Rituals do not make linear progress but are attuned to repetition and recall.

Ordinarily a community performs rituals collectively. This fact illustrates that rituals are effective in community building. Also beyond these formative aspects the effects of rituals endure in the community long after the ritual has ended. Community building roles are only one of the important roles of ritual, but they allow us to provide a preliminary definition. Rituals are formal patterns of behavior that unite and orient a group (or individual) toward a power that lies beyond them. That transcendent power must be understood in terms of a myth.

Australian Aboriginal Ritual

The study of Australian Aboriginal religions was once the great preserve of the timeless. Aboriginal Elders tell us that they had participated in 40,000 years of ritual Dreaming in their isolated continent. From this starting point the literal minded often jumped to conclusions. They thought the ceremonies observed in communities today would have been found identically the same 10,000, 20,000, perhaps 40,000 years ago, conducted by the same type of tribal leaders and for the same purposes. The Aboriginal Elders smiled at such a naïve conception. They knew better. Their Dreaming concept is far subtler, far more plastic.

Aboriginal Elders caution that the Dreaming should not be called Dreamtime, as if it were some static period, a time-out-of-mind before our phenomenal world began. Rather the

Dreaming is a creative period, an epoch when Dreaming Ancestors shaped and formed the earth as we know it today. Because this time was the source of all creativity, stories were to be told about what happened then and rituals were to be performed which remembered the activities of the Ancestral Beings of the Dreaming. There must be remembrance of the stories or the Dreaming would somehow be lost and with that loss would follow the loss of all meaning!

As the Elders well know, myths remember and rituals recreate. Without continual performance of appropriate rituals the power of the Ancestral Beings would no longer be available in the present to maintain the land. Yet landscapes do change. There can be no denial of that. Over centuries the sea rose and the Australian coasts were inundated. The land bridges between the Continent and the rest of Asia were cut. The ancient flora and fauna gave way to new forms that adjusted to new climatic conditions.

Last of all the 'whitefellers' came and profoundly changed the shape and uses of the land.[54] Along the way the ancient rituals also had to change. Of course they had to change without denying what they initially set out to do.

Changing rubrics to reinforce and not obscure remembrance is always a problem with ritual. It is the problem which a traditional Aboriginal Australian must face, and a problem for every traditionalist. How does he bring the past into the present without abandoning the past or denying the validity of the present? It is the problem of maintaining community over time, over generations.

It might be well to summarize the way in which Aboriginal Australians look upon ritual. They believe that participation in ceremonies will educate tribal members about the verities of life and about their own community, and so will serve to consolidate tribal unity. That in itself is not remarkable. Joining in ritual is a well-known means to enforce cohesion within a group, and to separate it from other groups. For Australian Aborigines the greatest significance of ritual is not in tribal unity. It lies rather in the powerful effect which the ceremonial has on the land, and on the cosmos. Ceremonies are important because they promote or follow up the Dreaming. These effects are not only local effects from the performance of rituals that were given to local groups. They flow from the performance of the many ceremonies, throughout the Australian Continent, which had been given to other Aboriginal communities by their Dreaming ancestors.

All members of an Aboriginal community need to know about the Dreaming activities of the Ancestral Beings who formed the world. But full participation and detailed knowledge is not a necessity for everyone. In Aboriginal communities many quite significant stories are never made public. These are only imparted selectively to a few trusted and mature individuals who have an inherited right to know them. It is enough that the Elders know them.

Younger adults and children are not expected to know very much about the secret Dreaming stories, but they can still take part in ritual even when their knowledge is fragmentary. Again not everyone is expected to take part, even in quite significant rituals. Indeed not everyone need know when or if they are being performed. It is sufficient if someone is performing them.

Western observers of Aboriginal rituals have emphasized the importance of the feelings, such as tribal solidarity and the creating of self-identity, elicited by ritual. But the larger question remains, what do these rituals do? For Aboriginal

Elders their rituals produce cosmic effect. Not that each and every ceremony has cosmic effects, but the important ones are supposed to shore up the world. Ritual activity preserves the world in its correct order, the order that was given by the Ancestral Being. Ritual activity recreates the Dreaming activity of the Ancestral Being. These rituals are not performed for the immediate benefit of the tribe, they are not functional, but rather they reflect a long-term care for the health of the land, its plants and animals.[55] Ritual renews the order laid down by the Ancestral Beings at the time of origins.

Specific rituals do have an immediate effect. For example, rituals of initiation have the immediate effect of incorporating a young man to be a full member of his particular community. Initiation rituals are expected to socialize an individual and to change him psychologically. Indeed, there is no lack of evidence that they do this. But even here, the more important purpose is to incorporate the individual into the life of the Ancestor. They aim to give the transcendent authority of the Ancestor new claims on the initiate.

Ceremonies are a source of power. They enable the initiate to approach and make use of the power of the Ancestral Beings who still reside in the land. This power is to be found most intensely in specific geographical places, where an Ancestral Being irrevocably entered the landscape when the Dreaming activity came to an end. Aboriginal rituals, not surprisingly, are typically related to these special locations, popularly known as sacred sites.

In Aboriginal religions rituals are central experiences. They channel the creative power of an Ancestor to individuals who have a right to be related to that Being, and they thus serve to unite a man or a woman to their universe. They affect the conscious mind to some extent, but it is equally obvious that they also affect the unconscious psyche. Rituals are forms of communication that transform and relocate an Aboriginal individual in the cosmos.

Ritual is a Form of Communication

Myths encapsulate the religious experience of a people. Taken together in the mythic cycle they describe events of cosmic importance. In pointing to a reality that lies beyond the myth they must communicate that reality indirectly through symbolic imagery. Myths must be remembered, but they must always be remembered in a controlled situation. For example Australian Aboriginal Elders are reluctant to allow their stories and ceremonies to be too well known, or to become known by inappropriate people. Any repetition of myth that draws the story too close to the surface of ordinary consciousness will cause it to loose its impact on the psyche. The myth will sink to the level of being mere information.

Myths are designed to facilitate our imperfect understanding, and they require the service of ritual to communicate the symbolic imagery and to maintain their hold on the unconscious psyche. Ritual through repetition associates memory with past events. Both the short-term memory of the participants in a ceremony and the long-term memories of the tribe are recalled.

Rituals communicate through performances. Normally the performances are before audiences. For, although it is said to be possible in Buddhist circles, it is difficult to think of a ritual conducted entirely within the privacy of ones' own mind. On the other hand, mere performance — going through the motions — does not constitute ritual. We have only to think of wedding rehearsals or practice for priestly ordination services. Every step of the ceremony may be executed to flawless perfection together with the appropriate gowns, vestments, and music; but no ritual has as yet taken place. At the end of the wedding rehearsal the individuals remain as unmarried as they were before.

Rituals communicate through patterned activity such as bowing while saying certain words or bowing before certain persons. But such activity is only ritualistic insofar as it communicates meaning. We have only to think of riding a bicycle, 'keeping the stroke' in rowing, or beating a drum to observe non-ritualistic patterned actions.

Elaborate patterned behavior can also be found in animals. For example the patterned mating behavior of birds has been filmed. This animal behavior is certainly communicative, but it only elicits unvarying instinctual responses. Therefore, in regard to the animal behavior, the word ritual must be taken metaphorically.

Ritual communicates through gesture and repetition. Drumming as a fanfare to introduce a leader, or breaking bread to begin a meal eaten in peace are examples of repetitious actions. Again, such repetitions and gestures become ritualized when they have been incorporated into meaningful action.

All these ritualistic actions can, of course, serve in more than one ritual. In these cases the specific behavior patterns can serve different scenarios and thus serve very different purposes

Four Elements of Ritual

As the Australian Aboriginal experience suggests rituals are complex phenomena that affect both individuals and groups in many ways at once. This complexity makes difficult the explanation of how rituals bring the past into the present.

There is a need to 'break them apart,' so to speak, to see how they function. But a tidy deconstruction is not available. It would be all too easy to take one characteristic of ritual, such as 'patterned activity,' and to construct an explanation around it. A second glance would show that our explanation gives only a partial grasp of how ritual works. With this warning in mind, and before attempting to relate ritual to the reality of myth we will discuss four significant aspects of ritual.

Attempts to discuss ritual in terms of one element or another without taking into account their complexity did much to impoverish appreciation of them in the recent past. This has left behind a legacy of reductionism and false problems that are only now being overcome. It was perhaps inevitable that before the age of tape-recorders and video cameras, students of ritual, especially rituals held in far distant places, should have concentrated their study on the texts and printed rubrics describing ceremonies.

The important elements found in ritual can be listed under four general headings: gesture, musical score, scene and story line. As noted, this is not to say that elements besides these four might not be isolated. However, these are the most prominent and are present in virtually all cases.

Under the general heading of gesture we can lump together all the various body movements that go on during ritual. This includes the movements both of individual performers and the community that is in attendance.

By score we understand music in its broadest sense, embracing melody, style and rhythmic cadence. Ritual score should be taken broadly to include forms of music that might not be immediately identified as such by the Western ear, but familiar enough in other cultures, such as rhythmic clapping or clicking.

Under the rubric of scene we, of course, put the type of location where a ritual is held, but the notion should be extended to include the decoration of the site, the timing of ritual and such things as special apparel worn by participants.

The story line, the last and most complex of the four elements, requires a special word of explanation. Story line should not be confused with the texts or the prayer formulas that accompany ritual actions. A didactic presentation may be rendered through the texts recited or sung while a gesture is performed. But what is found in written texts or even narratives learned by rote is not the only source of meaning in ritual. Meaning is transmitted through all the signs and symbols which rituals so freely employ. By the phrase, story line, we refer to the core meaning that is communicated in ritual through many instrumentalities.

Good rituals, the kind that have successfully retained their vitality over generations, contain these elements tightly bound together. Because ritual affects body as well as mind it is able to make a multi-level hidden impact. Rituals that fail to exploit all these avenues impoverish the process of interiorization of religious symbolism and eventually fade away. Examining these four elements more closely will show how they help bring the past into the present.

Gesture

As an element of ritual the formalized movements called gesture may involve those of solo performers up to a full panoply of processions and communal dancing. These unchanging, or relatively unchanging, movements may be

75

traditionally expected or legally required by the rubrics. Included here are the types of recurring and patterned activities carried on by performers at the conscious and semi-conscious level. In addition, gesture includes the more fluid movements that flow from the personal skills and ability of given performers. At times this will include their personal attitudes and feelings, and movements of the spirit.

On occasion, stylized gestures can be reduced to a type of sign language that communicates a precise and very conventional meaning. In this case the informed observer has nothing more to do than decode the conceptual meaning. Ritual gesture, however, is not to be taken as a language without benefit of words. When it is needed to communicate information gestures are less useful than texts.

Ritual gesture communicates in quite a different way than text because it has the ability to orchestrate shifts of mood and feeling in audiences or congregations. Gesture moves below the surface of consciousness to bind emotional life to the ritual events. A skilled or emotionally charged performer may graft a personal and idiosyncratic experience of life onto the on-going life of the community. Gesture contributes powerfully to the goal of the ritual because it mediates an understanding of the symbolic meaning of the ritual. While gesture should not be mistaken for ritual, rituals cannot do without gesture and still retain the ritual mode of communication.

Ritual gestures can, and do, change. In approaching a mystery that is beyond our ken there is obviously a latitude in the understanding to be communicated. There is, as we know:

> a time to mourn and a time to dance; a time for embracing and a time to refrain from embracing; a time for gathering stones together and a time for

casting stones aside; a time of war and a time for peace[56]

As the mood of a community changes, gestures must also change if meaning is to be made clear. Even more so, if the membership of a community changes, gestures must change. Such changes can only be accomplished successfully, however, if the gesture remains recognizable within the new ritual context.

Scene

The importance of scene to ritual is often set aside or entirely forgotten. However, scene adds immeasurably to the social dimension of ritual.

The importance of a specific place, the sacred site, in connection with Aboriginal ceremonies has been made clear. Many Aboriginal ceremonies cannot be conducted outside their proper site. Ritual events are communal events. They are designed to be conducted in communal locations such as temples, churches, dancing grounds, caves and the like. Place evokes memories of who was there in the past, effecting a kind of re-incarnation. Place reminds us of what was done there in the past, fleshing out the bare bones of remembrance of past deeds. But other aspects of scene are important too.

The materials used to set the scene for a ritual cannot be chosen at random. The clothing, seating arrangements, lighting, even colors are more than arbitrary decoration. Nor can lecterns, altars, chairs, lamp stands, sacred poles, and other elements be moved around like it were living room furniture. A scene must be set in accord with the needs of ritual itself and arranged to convey the appropriate meaning. To fail to do so is to run the risk of detaching the ambience of a space from its ritual meaning. For example in Western Christian liturgies the smoke of burning incense signifies the presence of the Deity. In Australian Aboriginal rituals smoke is a signal that purification and healing is taking place.

Scene, like gestures, sometimes have to change. A scene dominated by a setting appropriate to the past can bring to bear a crushing weight on the present. Catholic ritualists discovered this when they tried to carry out rituals employing guitars, modern folk tunes and a kiss of peace within the formal setting of a Gothic cathedral. Changing the position of the altar, or the location of rails and pews can nullify the ritual in the eyes of many. So great is the loss of identity with such changes that some do not return to the ritual. Architecture makes its statement long after the builders have left!

Adjustment of scene is a delicate matter. However the vitality of a ritual will often depend upon how well the modified scene will allow the past associations of the community to be integrated with the present. A community has at once a present, a past, and a future. An effective ritual must embrace all three.

Score

Scene is important because of its ability to evoke communal associations, while musical score, like gesture, has importance because it is so closely linked to meaning. Students of liturgical performance are usually well aware of the significance of musical score. They recognize that music is an essential part of the 'packaging' of meaning. Curiously enough though, it is an element that is often slighted in academic and theological discussions of ritual. Perhaps that common phrase, musical accompaniment, is much to blame.

It should be remembered that music is never mere accompaniment. When we move beyond a strictly cerebral level it is music that bears much of the burden of generating meaning. This becomes immediately evident when we think of musical score in relation to gesture. Without music the patterned movements of ballet dancers seem ridiculous — except perhaps to the few experts who can grasp, in an abstract way, the formal patterns in the dancers' steps.

Score can both carry or impede what a ritual is trying to express. In skillful hands celebrations can blend organ, guitar, choral elements, and exotic instruments to form a cultural unity. On the other hand, if the principal concern is to 'give everyone a go' the result can be chaotic. Where competing musical values are left to run unchecked a ritual looses its impact.

While the close relationship between gesture and score is well recognized, the intimate relation of score and text is sometimes overlooked. A common expectation is that the text will bear the burden of transmitting meaning. Yet in significant ways music modifies and interprets what a text will say. This is particularly clear in screen plays.

Contemporary culture recognizes the impact of music in films, television dramas, and other media events where the background music is charged with conveying a variety of information. A shift of cadence warns that danger lurks behind a door. The ethos of a character can be built up by shifts from chord to chord, and the audience find themselves identifying with the character's journey. A shift from C-major to E-major leads our psyche to expect the character in question to sing of courage and strength, or that he will be courageous and strong in the future.

Music also enters into our consciousness more deeply than simply raising apprehension or signaling the arrival of the hero. Organizers who stage shows such as 'Heavy Metal' or Madonna concerts and the police who monitor the concerts are aware of the power that music exercises over a crowd. The sensitivity of illustrious musicians, such as Mozart and Verdi made them acutely aware of the possibilities of a musical key and the powers of melody to physically affect the human psyche.[57] The love arias of Mozart were routinely written in E flat major.[58] Music with repeated perfect fifths exudes confidence, strength, and optimism. Stephen Spielberg used this technique in his very popular films Star Wars and E.T. The musical score, in fact, overcame the shortcomings of his stories which were pedestrian and unlikely candidates to capture the popular imagination. Persons leaving the theater after the Spielberg productions felt confident and uplifted about life in the Universe. This was not because of the story they had been told, but because the music had reached below their cerebral consciousness to their emotions.

As listeners we are empowered to share in the genius of a Mozart or the energy of a Madonna though we are unable to create it ourselves. Music affects both the individual and the community, and has the power to draw a community together. Though not always recognized, these dynamics operate within religious ritual.

Story line

As has already been suggested the mere reading of text should not be confused with the story line. There is a time and place for reading content in ritual, but story line includes much more than text.

Unfortunately the concept story line is sometimes confused with what is recited while gesticulations are going on. This leads to the assumption that ritual is essentially a cerebral exercise, that it is something on the order of a dramatic reading of a lesson. Where this attitude prevails there is an impoverishment of the ritual, a weakening of story line. By themselves the formulas, prayers and hymns that are part of the ritual communicate meaning in a conceptual manner. Whether long or short, read badly or brilliantly, such texts do not produce the full impact that a ritual is designed to achieve.

An examination of the use of oral texts in Australian Aboriginal ceremonies is illuminating. In these rituals words are not called upon to carry much of the message. To outside observers the words spoken or chanted, shorn of the context of gesture and score, leave a very cryptic impression, to say the least.

Visitors present at the performance of Aboriginal rituals often ask their neighbor for a translation of the words being sung in order to acquire some better understanding of what they are witnessing, only to be nonplused by the spare replies they are given. Three or four words may be whispered to them, words that seem to mean virtually nothing at all. The meager responses lead observers to think they have not been told the whole truth, or that the Aboriginal translator has an imperfect command of English; when, in fact, they are being told all there is to say.

In one extreme case the song, sung by the Aboriginal performer, consisted of a single proper noun repeated in a number of keys and rhythms. The name referred to a group of human/spirit beings whose identity and activities were well known in the neighborhood, thus proposing endless possible implications for local listeners. The scene, score and gesture accompanying the word would limit or embellish the meanings that were appropriate.

The fact is that the bare texts of Aboriginal rituals, without accompanying music and dancing, carry very little of the story line. This gives Aboriginal communities a distinct advantage in maintaining the secret character of their rituals. They can politely permit outsiders to be present and overhear the whole of a ceremony without, on that account, surrendering its inner meaning. The inner meaning is kept secret from outsiders and the uninitiated as something not suitable for profane ears. It also enables children to be present and to witness, and even share in the ritual life of their people without being prematurely exposed to inner mysteries which are considered appropriate only for those who are older.

These rituals, nevertheless, still make a powerful impact both in the Aboriginal community and on those who come in contact with them. Possession of a text, and obviously to a greater degree possession of only a translation of a text, does not enable one to know what a ritual ultimately implies. In the final analysis the story line is found in the broader context of the cycle of myths that are accepted and believed in a community. Story line is drawn from the memories and the understandings of the culture preserved in mind and heart.

Further considerations reinforce the notion that the meaning of a ritual cannot be reduced to bare texts. First, individual performers may over the years muddle the words or even forget them. Secondly, participants may not have had explicit knowledge of a ritual in the first place. Yet they still participate — even vigorously — in a ritual activity. Thirdly communities can seemingly loose sight of the meaning of a ritual and still continue to be devoted to it.

If the memory of the story line is lost why is a ritual continued? A number of reasons are commonly put forward. The ritual is being re-enacted routinely now because an authority once commanded it and the voice of that authority is still respected. It is continued out of a kind of lethargy – 'it is something which we have always done.' Outside factors may be alleged. The ritual provides a convenient opportunity for the community to get together, or more simply, a number of individuals find it an enjoyable thing to do. Such reasons may be offered, but more likely the ritual is being re-enacted because its meaning, despite appearances, is still alive. The symbolism is still present and active below the surface levels of consciousness. Meaning is still being expressed and transmitted through the less obvious elements of ritual.

While loss of a detailed understanding of the story line will produce a ritual that may be defective, that will not necessarily stop re-enactment of the ritual. Rituals whose meanings are completely lost will be allowed to slide into oblivion.

The Unity of Ritual

Historically there has been excessive concentration on narrative in the study of rituals. Concentrating on any one element to the exclusion of others will give rise to problems. In fact, it appears that it is possible to have a true ritual without any accompanying verbal formula, and even a ritual without a story line. Accompanying words may be unnecessary where the score and scene communicate the story line to a particular community. These types of theoretical problems were taken up by the Australian anthropologist W. E. H. Stanner during his meticulous examination of Murrinh-patha rituals:

> On the other hand, examination of gestures without reference to the narrative is not helpful. In

the past field workers have given truly bizarre meanings to rituals based on their observation of dances and ceremonies. These mischaracterizations should be warnings against attempting to interpret rituals before understanding the language and history of the community, or by assuming the rituals are somehow products of gesture alone.[59]

Scene is also an element that cannot be taken in isolation. By themselves, comparisons between the shapes of temples from different centuries will not reveal much; comparisons of the wall paintings in caves from different regions cannot be expected to tell us a great deal. Archaeological finds without context will reveal little or nothing about rituals performed at these locations. Discussions of Australian Aboriginal ancient rock paintings are examples of the latter difficulty. These discussions have suffered from attempts to draw conclusions from what was mere happenstance or accidental in styles.

Indeed, even the significance of location can be difficult to interpret. The concept of location varies from religion to religion. For some, the site for performing a ritual can be simply a matter of convenience – what does it matter which chapel is used? what significance can there be in the location of the dancing ground? For others, the site of the ritual performance is interlocked with the structure of the myth. In aboriginal religions it is quite impossible to perform a ritual if the 'scene' is wrong. No amount of 'going through the motions' will be of any avail if the ceremony is performed outside the appropriate sacred place.

The fact that the four elements of ritual form a unity does not mean that each element must be given equal weight. Religions of the book naturally emphasize story line, and shape their rituals by interspersing sacred texts throughout. Religions tied to the natural landscape have looked to gesture, musical score, and scene. Australian Aboriginal rites are sometimes placed where rock formations form a natural echo chamber. However, while emphases may differ, the elements of a ritual can not be studied in isolation without doing violence to the understanding of the ritual.

Ritual in Relation to Myth

Both ritual and myth are symbolic expressions of hidden arcana – a hidden mystery. The mysteries of the cosmos will always remain beyond our ken. Nevertheless, myths and rituals can mediate something of them to our understanding, to our emotions and unconscious life through the rhythms of our bodily life.

Not every ritual need have a supporting myth that stands in a one-to-one relationship with its gesture and verbal formula. In many rituals words are not spoken, and a myth may not even be brought to conscious mind. For medieval theologians the close union of words with ritual gesture was typical only of a limited class of rituals called sacraments. For example, when the action of pouring water on the head of a person was conjoined with reciting a Trinitarian formula the result was a ritual known as the sacrament of Baptism.

While a close union of myth and gesture is not the case in every ritual, nevertheless, a ritual has a story line. The story line is found in the cycle of myths known and remembered in the community.

Ritual and Community

Rituals can never be fully isolated from the religious experiences of the community that formed them. The story line must involve both the nature-symbolism shared by the whole of humanity, and also the love of nature generated by the local symbols. So the story line will incorporate symbolism from nature such as fire, air, or water; and from the natural landscape such as hills, rivers, or plains of the particular land the community inhabits. Thus the river Jordan, the Sinai Desert, and the cities of Rome and Jerusalem will always figure in the Christian context. While Ulurú and the Victoria River will forever figure in the Australian Aborigine context.

The story line will also include the historical symbols that arose from a community's past religious experiences. For example, Australian Aborigines will draw symbols from that history grounded in the stories of their sacred ancestors. For Christians symbolism will be found in the history of salvation drawn from the sacred Scriptures. Rituals and myths are designed to communicate a distinctive interpretation of experience. Rituals thus enable a community to act out what they cannot otherwise articulate.

The question arises, what is the group for which rituals are conducted. They are obviously conducted as a service to the men, women and children gathered at a time and place. They accomplish their initial purpose if they organize and unify the minds, emotions and psyche of the members of that group. This is in itself no mean purpose, but it is hardly all that is commonly expected of ritual.

No community is composed solely of its present company. An ephemeral crowd of individuals thrown together by happenstance may not have a vision beyond the day. A community must look beyond the present moment; it must have roots and a future. The religious roots of a community lie in an interpretation of experience that it has been led to accept over time. If the community is cut off from that history it will wither and die.

Bringing the Past into the Present

Ritual forms and shapes a community by bringing its religious history, its particular past, into the present. The communication effected by ritual is not simply given at the linguistic or conceptual level. It involves imagination, the sensual, and the biological side of nature. Rituals have the power to evoke the collective memories of the group. Through ritual both natural and historical symbolism is introduced to the unconscious. There the symbolism will be repeated again and again.

If ritual is to be affective it must bring the past into the present, not as an antiquarian recollection of events, but as a living presence. The religious community to which ritual speaks is not restricted to the company present, or to the members in the past, or to all of them taken together. Rather, the ritual must bring into the present that creative principle which created the first place.

In an Aboriginal ritual the most important person asked to be present is the Dreaming Ancestor. It is that power and not the power of the group that is made available. In Christian rituals the most significant person present at the ritual gathering is Christ, whom Christians believe to be the Son of God. It is his life and history, which their ritual brings into the present, not as a heroic, historical person, but as mediating an experience of the presence of God. Around this person every Christian community must form. It is because of the presence of this person believers confidently expect that their rituals will have power.

Flight from Rituals

Clearly rituals will affect some people differently than they affect others. For some their psyche will be deeply affected. Others will be attuned primarily to the story line, or the musical score, or the scene. Enthusiasm for ritual has waxed and waned as societies changed. In the present times there is a failure to appreciate the function of ritual and a flight from it in religious and secular settings.

Authors as different as Mary Douglas and Lyman Gilkey have reported the flight from ritual.[60] The time given to participating in ritual and the care in preparing them has been reduced since the 1960's. Reduction in quantity of ritual has been matched by a reduction in quality. There is a flight from ritual within the rituals themselves. The formal and more rubrical elements in ceremonies have been deemphasized and shortened.

Catholic religious services, which in the Western tradition have been the most ritualistic, are a good example of the loss of ritual. In comparison with the past, the Mass, the central rite in Catholicism, is now a wordier affair. The Eucharistic prayers, in the past called canons, that were introduced in the 1960's gave careful expression to the story line of the Eucharist. But they did so in a somewhat cerebral manner and were embellished with far fewer ceremonial gestures than heretofore. The vestments of the officiants have been simplified. The decorations about the altar have been reduced. In addition, layers of cloths that covered the sacred vessels are no longer used. The scene also was modified by reorganizing the church interiors. These things were done in the service of intelligibility, but the total impact of the ritual was reduced. The attendance at Eucharistic rituals declined notably following these changes.

A sign of the decline of ritual impact was the need for more planning. Story line no longer matched easily with gesture, score, and scene. Services no longer proceeded automatically but had to be planned. Courses for planning ceremonies became popular in seminaries. These courses, sometimes called Presidential Style, outline the different ways that ceremonies can be constructed and carried out.

A need is now felt to plan creative liturgies that do not follow familiar ritual patterns. This raises the question, is this simply a call for change of gesture and score to reinforce the presentation of the story line, or is it the creation of something entirely new because the original story line has been lost?

Examples of the flight from ceremonies could be multiplied. Another sign of the flight from ritual can be found in families that leave old neighborhoods. All too often they jettison their attendance at church with the change in lifestyle. What may be more significant, this is often done with little sense of loss and without a conscious decision. With the current deafness to myths the meaning of religious symbolism falls on deaf ears.

If rituals are so important why is there currently a flight from ritual? A popular answer is that the loss of ritual is a reflection of the dysfunction of present society. As a society becomes strained, the argument runs, many of its old values and attitudes toward life will no longer seem relevant to a larger and larger percent of people. The symbols and the ceremonies, which reflected the values of an older order, lose their hold on the psyche. Rituals, which were designed to inculcate and reinforce the values of the old order, will seem to be more and more simply formal exercises done for 'old times sake'. The old times appear less and less relevant to modern life. With confusion in the collective values of the community there is naturally a desire for new ritual expressions that will be more personal and more ethical in approach. In other words, there will be a desire for new ceremonies to meet a new community's needs.

Indeed rituals have assuredly not disappeared and, in fact, show signs of a revival. It is not necessarily a bad sign that planning for religious worship is in some ways a more serious affair than heretofore. Liturgies which in the past proceeded too automatically now need to be planned beforehand, sometimes days beforehand. While the need for ritual is recognized there is increasing lack of knowledge about rituals and what they are supposed to do. The answer to the question of what they are supposed to do lies in myth and in the symbolism by which it is articulated.

CHAPTER VII

MYTH AND SYMBOLISM

Symbolizing can be described in general terms as the substitution of one image for another in the service of greater knowledge. Ernst Cassirer known for his work on symbolic forms has remarked that human beings are symbolizing animals — and who can disagree with him?[61]

Religious myths have a special character because their symbolic language points beyond themselves to things not known by ordinary means. These myths that appear simple enough at first, are stories that cannot be understood if taken at face value.

Symbols and Signs

Symbols are not to be confused with simple, one-dimensional signs. A placard on a wall showing a lighted cigarette enclosed in a red circle with a diagonal line drawn is a sign. It is not a symbol. This picture is an international sign meaning simply that smoking is not allowed. No other meaning is intended. A stained glass window showing a Catherine Wheel next to a woman draped in classical clothes tells us that the woman represented there is Saint Catherine of Alexandria, and not, for example, Catherine of Siena. The Sienese saint is shown with a lily and a somewhat drawn and pallid face indicating that in her life she fasted a lot. Although the stained glass panel may be in a church, it is not a symbol. It is simply a sign referring us to one thing — St. Catherine of Alexandria and how she died.

Religious paintings use a certain amount of conventional imagery as well imagery from religious rituals and myths. Such conventional imagery is sometimes called symbolic, even though once their meanings have been explained they can be read off straightforwardly. In our usage those conventions will be considered signs. Like the no smoking sign, the stained glass panel is intended to say only one thing, behold the martyr, Catherine of Alexandria. It is an example of language without words — language quite independent of the spoken language of the person viewing it.

Religious myths, in addition to their symbolic language, include imagery that has simple sign value of the type described above. Sorting out the sign values of religious language is a matter of simple translation. Signs present no special problems about being grounded in reality.

Religious myths also deal with mysteries. They communicate an understanding of what can never be fully understood. Religious myths are concerned with the mystery of God and the action of God on humanity and the cosmos. While myths use stories that can be read or listened to easily enough, their language in dealing with mystery must be interpreted in a symbolic manner.

The Problem of Grounding Myth in Reality

Often the use of symbols means to the non-poetic soul the substitution of the less known, the more obscure, for a clear and distinct idea. When applied to religion, symbolism may seem to overlay a secondary meaning to an image or a story that was clear enough in the first place. The symbolic relation appears to saddle the story with an alternative interpretation that seems more nebulous and historically less plausible. Sometimes even believers wonder if the use of religious symbolism is not simply mystification.

Religious symbols are usually justified to the skeptical by the plea that symbols permit us to gaze into the unknown and to penetrate a mystery that exceeds our ability to fathom in any other way. Students of religion have long struggled with the problem of symbolism, and over the content which religious symbols claim to have. As substitutions for empirical discussions symbols are always going to be obscure in some way. That much can be readily agreed to. But the question remains, do they have independent intellectual content beyond those elements that were originally present in the sacred stories in the first place?

It is possible to approach symbolizing from many points of view, not all of which can be looked into here.[62] It will not be possible to pursue the investigations initiated so fruitfully by C. G. Jung and his followers. Jung traced the impact symbols have on both the personal and collective unconscious and found a universality of content in the unconscious that validated his use of symbolism. Authors of widely differing points of view, such as the late Mircea Eliade, Joseph Campbell and Wilhelm Schmidt, took another line of approach that will be bypassed. They made voluminous catalogues of myths in an effort to trace the origin and diffusion of religious symbolism. For quite different reasons their research convinced them that universality could be claimed for symbols in many areas of life. The approach adopted by writers Emile Durkheim and Bronislaw Malinoski will also be bypassed. These writers examined the social and functional role of group behavior in generating religious symbolism.[63]

Those approaches will be set aside because our concern is not particularly about the psychological origin and social function of symbolism. Our concern will be with religious symbols themselves. To what do religious symbols refer? If they refer to something spiritual is it a content beyond ordinary experience? What grounds do religious symbols have for saying what they do? To examine these questions let us turn to Christian authors and explore what they had to say.

Christian Approaches to Symbolism

Scripture says God is a spirit "who must be worshipped in spirit and truth."[64] Christian thinkers are aware of the necessity to use symbolic and indirect expressions when referring to God. To avoid covert idolatry, language has to be used with care to prevent anthropomorphisms from creeping in inadvertently. Visual imagery and concepts have to be indirect when talking about God. This is true both in conducting public prayers and discussions and in meditating on God in the privacy of one's own mind.

Christians learned from their Jewish 'forebears' that it was impossible, as well as beside the point, to attempt to transmit concrete information about God. God is pure spirit! Whatever else this may mean, it means that God is Other. Jewish and Christian traditions agree on this point with philosophers from ancient Greece. The three traditions insist that the divine nature transcends material categories. God is not up in the heavens any more than down on the earth for the obvious reason that only material objects can be located in a place. It is simply not appropriate to ask about size, time or location of God. References in Scripture to the hands, feet or breath of God were simply poetic metaphors. In the ancient traditions persons relegated materially descriptive phrases to casual conversation, but only the unlearned or pagans would actually take such expressions literally. Demythologizing has a very ancient history!

The Christian doctrine of Incarnation has not altered matters. Church councils have taught that Christ was 'hypostatically united to the Word in the Trinity.' This phrase is used to convey a description of the mystery of Christ as two natures in one person – each mature, complete, and intact.[65] Therefore, it was perfectly correct to make the statement, 'Jesus Christ is God.' But at the same time the faithful understood that the human nature of Jesus was something that had been created. The physical flesh and bones were things formed in time and were not eternal. Even the human mind of Christ with its attractive personality traits was created and then formed in his family and conditioned by the culture of first century Judaism.

Reflection on the mystery of the Incarnation made thoughtful individuals realize that the elect might see the glorified body of Christ with human eyes, but even the elect in heaven would not see God with physical vision. To ask if someone would look on the face of God in the literal sense of the phrase was precisely to ask a meaningless question. The use of such a phrase must be understood in some symbolic sense.

The birth of Christ did not change human inability to touch the divine nature as such. Those who had been privileged to see him might describe the human body of Jesus in physical terms. A historical account could be given of the events of his life. But these descriptions told of the humanity of Christ, not about the nature of his divinity.

While it seems obvious to theologians and to other thoughtful persons that the divine nature can never be the direct object of sense experience, there is an ancient, equally powerful conviction running through Christian thought that human beings can know God — even in this present life. Granted that such knowledge might be very imperfect and incomplete compared with the vision of God reserved to the saints, there is, nevertheless, some perception of the divine nature — of the Godhead - possible here and now. Admittedly, Jewish tradition gave this idea a much less warm reception. God was unknown, only his will for us is open to our inspection.[66]

The Psalms say, "The heavens declare the glory of God and the firmament proclaims his handiwork."[67] At the same time, Christians do not equate knowledge of the cosmos, however elevated, with knowledge of God. What might be the content of our knowledge of God, or how our ideas referred to God was a major concern for speculative theologians over the centuries. With speculation came precision and nuance as well.

Theologians counseled that experiencing the worldly effects of divine power did not imply that one knew the nature of that power — any more than knowing the path to a goal meant knowing the goal itself. Knowing God's will did not mean knowing the God who authored it. Christianity accepted that the Scriptures are the key that unlocks the mystery of the divine plan for human history. But familiarity with the plan for human history does not mean knowing the divine mind behind it. The saints were admired for their holiness, but human conduct however exalted is a human way of being. God's way of being is quite other.

The Apophatic Way

If nothing in the created universe, even the physical body of the Christ, was like divine nature; how then is it possible, to come to any knowledge of the inner life and nature of God? Faced with this problem, a highly influential fifth century theologian Denis the Areopagite accepted the view that knowledge of God was impossible in this life. All that could be said even armed with Scripture, was to state what God was not.[68] Symbolic language was no exception to this rule.

Denis' point of view has always had a significant following, but his apophatic way of speaking did not seem to be entirely satisfactory. Especially in the West, there was a firmly rooted conviction that human beings really did possess an understanding of God grounded somehow through earthly imagery. A close study of nature; a perceptive observation of the human conduct of saints and sinners; an awareness of the special relationship of the Jews and the Church; could not all these things form a basis for learning about the inner being of God? Many theologians and spiritual authors answered yes.

The Likeness of God in Creation

While God is a spirit that transcends creation, there are many passages in Scripture that suggested God is, nonetheless, somehow like creation. The opening chapter of Genesis announced that God had made human beings in his image and likeness! So some knowledge of God could be based on human similarity, even if nothing else was found in the rest of creation. This notion was reinforced by Saint Paul in a passage that became a proof-text for those who wished to argue the point. In discussing the moral culpability of pagans who lived before the Gospel, he said that ignorance about God could not be an excuse for their sinful behavior. Saint Paul's argument was, since the creation of the world, invisible realities and God's eternal power and divinity, had been visible through the things he made. Sinful pagans were inexcusable, since they certainly had knowledge of God.[69]

Saint Augustine agreed with Saint Paul, but made a distinction that became standard in the West.[70] He argued that God appeared in the things he made in two ways. First, He appeared in a general likeness found in the physical world. Secondly, He appeared more clearly in the special likeness found in the most perfect material work of God's creation — human nature.

It became customary for exegetes to say that the material world disclosed a trace, or a vestige, of the divinity whereas the rational mind yielded up an image of God — the imago Dei.[71]

Pondering over images and vestiges of God found in creation did not produce any crude pictorial representations of God to be sure. That would have been crass idolatry! Rather it enabled meditative men and women to discern a likeness. These likenesses were open to persons of every age and in every place. They were open to believers and non-believers alike as they mulled over their experience of God. The vestiges and image of God in creation generated symbols that were cosmic and transcultural for all to embrace.[72]

The understanding of God gained in this way is important since it enables thoughtful persons to become aware of an abiding supernatural presence in the universe. However, the insights gained are so general and so imprecise that they can be easily interpreted in various ways. They have, in fact, been pressed into the service of many different religions. Symbolism of a cosmic character is what pagans, ancient and modern, continually rediscover in their religious meandering and which they incorporate into their religions — not always correctly. The clouded and uncertain knowledge of God gained from meditating on the vestiges found in nature can be dangerous for they can become little more than a celebration of the rhythms of biological life and earthly desires. This kind of search for God terminates all too often in the sum of human aspirations projected uncritically upon the sky.[73]

The Likeness of God using Scriptures

Sacred histories also provide a base for symbolism. In Judeo-Christian communities the sacred writings of the Jews offer a much deeper insight into the divine than vagaries gathered from the world of nature. Beginning with ancient Israel and continuing with the New Israel, religions of the book see a self disclosure of God in a series of historical events that shaped God's chosen people. The choosing of Abraham; the calling of Israel out of Egypt into the Promised Land; the Exile from that Holy Land; the Exile itself; and the return to the Holy Land, were events dear to the Jewish people. Flowing out of these events came the announcement to Mary of the coming of Christ; the salvific actions of Christ's life, death, and resurrection; and the formation of the Church; these were events dear to the Christian community. All of these events and many minor ones were regarded as interventions by God that formed a sacred mysterious history. This history was like others in the ancient Middle East and in one sense was not particularly remarkable. However, it depended on the actions of God and was symbolic because it pointed beyond itself.

By meditating upon this history hearers could acquire an understanding of the life of Israel and the early church, which could be called the life of God in history. This history had meanings at many levels. Its many actors, such as Jacob, Joseph,

Samuel, Ruth, King David, John the Baptist, and what happened to them in time acquired allegorical value.

In this sacred history the past was often laid as a mantle over the future. For example, readers of the history in looking back might notice frequent stories about unusual and miraculous births that occurred at decisive turning points for Israel. The stories of the births of Isaac, Samuel, and John the Baptist; as well the story of the birth, prophesied by Isaiah, of the desired child to be born of a virgin; were all unusual births. In consequence, the idea that the Messiah would enter history upon the occasion of an extraordinary birth was recognized as following a theme. The symbol of the unusual birth would be in keeping with the divine plan. It would foreshadow the claim made in the Prologue of John's Gospel that the "Word was made flesh and dwelt among us"[74]

The history of Israel recorded in her sacred writings was interlaced with many themes, interlocking events, that referred to aspects of an apparent plan. God, who was ultimately responsible for all events, had determined the sequence of events. Therefore Israel's history carried a hidden meaning. It was a storehouse of symbolism that enabled readers to grasp something of God's way of being. There is evidence to show that early Church Fathers marshaled such themes from biblical and non-biblical literature.[75]

Themes traced over the centuries through many books of the Bible became the exegetical basis for unraveling its many levels of meaning. Cosmic symbols, the vestiges of God discovered in the book of nature, were relegated to second place. As was the custom of the Jewish rabbis the likenesses found in history became primary. They were prized as more precise and personal because they were built by successive acts of divine initiative and given to a people prepared to receive them. Interpretations of the Glossators over Scripture became very constant and traditional with time.[76]

Not everything given in Scripture is celebrated, however. Not all the qualities attached to biblical heroes are worthy. Craftiness, for example, was a character trait of King David. He was much admired, but his craftiness remained a human trait and not one attributed to God. Marriage was an important aspect in the divine life of the gods of other nations but the god of Israel had no spouse. Symbolism is more than mere allegory.

Study of Biblical themes showed that historical symbolism was not without ambiguity. After all, the synagogue and the church do not interpret identical Scriptural texts in the same way. The theme of the Temple is important to both communities, but as a symbol it has a different meaning for each of them. The emerging Christian community saw all the events of Sacred history foreshadowing the coming of Christ, the synagogue did not. The Mishnah and the Talmud are examples of different symbolic systems. Also reinterpretation of the texts can be seen where Christian ministers simply treat the stories of battles and violent warfare sprinkled throughout the Psalms and Prophets as allegories for the struggles of the soul against sin. Tracing appropriate themes and drawing correct applications would be the constant preoccupation of the guardians of tradition!

The Character of Cosmic and Historical Symbols

Cosmic symbols are considered a 'baser coin'. Lustrations using water and oil for strengthening could be found in almost every tribe or culture. These give glimpses of the divine power, drawn from nature or from shrewd observation of conventional human behavior. This is to be contrasted with the more precise and personal symbols in sacred histories of the Jews or of the treks of the Dreaming ancestors of the Australian Aborigines in 'time out of mind.'

The historical imagery, however, carries a burden. It can appear arbitrary, enigmatic, irrational, and forced. If the flow of sacred history followed a plan orchestrated by God, then the likenesses of God drawn from it were artificial constructions, albeit God was believed to be the artificer. Only someone privileged to know the correct line of interpretation could uncover the proper meaning embedded in sacred history. Interpretations of Israel's history by the early Church seemed, to outsiders at any rate, to rest on retrospective or quixotic readings of events. When Aboriginal Elders give interpretations of Dreaming stories they attract the same criticism.

Are the meanings assigned to events in sacred history simply a way of putting the best face on a checkered chronicle? Is historical symbolism a canonization of patterns that have proved successful? Like myths that celebrated the rhythms of biological life, is sacred history an idealized story -- an ideal pattern 'projected on the sky?' It cannot be argued here whether such projections were ever made. I will only note two factors concerning Israel's history that mitigated against this. First, when acting in history the plan of God had a constant purpose in view. Its symbolism looked to the future, to a succession of disclosures to be fulfilled in the time of the Messiah. Israel's history did not try to return to an idealized past, and in that sense did not look for an idealized pattern 'projected on the sky.' Secondly, when Christians came to draw symbols from sacred history they essentially adopted the view that salvation, the goal of sacred history, was fulfilled in Christ. The time of Christ was a time to return to and celebrate, but it was at the same time a point of departure for the work of salvation not yet carried out. The Church looked to the future, to the Second Coming, when all things would be new again.

With the end of the Apostolic Age divine disclosure was complete. His immediate followers in the Church added nothing extraneous to the work of Christ. In that sense sacred history had come to an end. The storehouse of symbolism was now filled up. The task for the future was to "contend for the faith which was once and for all delivered to the saints."[77]

Historic symbolism would now look back to apostolic age to ground its allegories and analogies. Cosmic symbolism would still find a place but it would need to be harmonized with sacred history.

Religious Symbolism and Reality

It is time to return now to the initial questions. What do religious symbols refer to? and how are they grounded in reality?

At the outset it is clear that God, the ultimate object of religious symbols, is a reality that exceeds human understanding. God is the fullness of being. Any defect in our knowledge of God lies in the weakness of human intellect to fathom the fullness — to comprehend the possibilities — of being. The human mind can never grasp reality from the divine point of view.

Although there is more intelligibility in God than can be compressed into any creature, nevertheless creatures must be our starting point for grounding symbolism. This is the case since creatures are the only objects lying within the normal range of our experience. Because of this limitation we will never find a likeness to God in a comprehensive way in creation. However, creatures can point to levels of intelligibility that exceed what is in them. There is nothing innately illogical in drawing metaphors from human and material created objects. We must begin with creatures if we want to ground symbolism in reality![78]

The Framework for Religious Language

It is one thing to believe that symbolic language is necessary to speak about God. It is quite another matter to show that such language exists.

Saint Augustine gave an explanation of how symbolic language arises and why it is a valid mode of expression. His explanation endured a long time reaching into the Middle Ages. For Augustine the world we live in is a world of limitation and change. No perfect or absolute truth can be found there. Everything is subject to change and decay, and will inevitably dissolve into its parts. Only God is simple, immutable, and immune from change. Any understanding we have of truth, of goodness, or of timelessness must derive from a realm of truth, goodness, and timelessness. For Augustine symbolism is grounded in the eternal ideas existing in the mind of God.[79] The material cosmos of itself is incapable of any sort of stasis, and after the sin of Adam and Eve the instability of the cosmos increased. A deeper state of uncertainty set in. Yet even in its weakened state creation reflects a limited likeness to divine reality. God continues to be the exemplar of all things, since all things are patterned after the exemplary ideas in the mind of God. Using present day terminology, the exemplary ideas act as parameters within which created things find their identity and individuality.

In Augustine's analysis likeness is found at three levels:

1. There is a likeness or an idea existing in the mind of God. This likeness is perfect and a complete expression of the ideal.

2. There is a likeness existing in created individuals. The likeness in individuals is a reflection of the exemplar. It has a lesser reality – a mere participation in the divine idea.

3. There is a likeness known by the human mind. This likeness is an imitation of the ideal.

The three likenesses are similar in the sense they each offer the same understanding, but each at its own level.

The purpose of symbolic language was to draw the human mind, the minds of believers and non-believers alike, to awareness of the exemplar form. Symbolism drew the human mind to the ideal existing in God from the imperfect suggestions of it found in the created world. At the same time, symbols led the human mind to an experience of God as reflected in the mirror of one's own consciousness. Everyone has some experience of the ideal. But for Augustine Divine illumination was the agency that made the fuller extent of these likenesses evident to human mind. Although incapable of exhausting the Divine idea fully in this way a meditative person could grasp the likenesses that were implicit in created temporal reality.[80]

Armed with the explanation of how the likeness of the Divine nature was reflected in the cosmos, in the human soul, in the imago dei, and in sacred history; both exegetes and laity felt at ease in using symbolic language. The referent of symbols was the participation that humans had in the divine ideas. Some theologians were content to speak of human ideas as copies, or reflections of the divine ideas without looking into the matter more closely.

A serious issue was unresolved however – what of the vast abyss that stretched between the reality of God and the unreality of creation? How did the idea of a vast abyss match with the notion that God and creation were supposed to be related as an original and a likeness? These divine and earthly realms were not merely examples of more and less. If God is totally other, it would be closer to the truth to say that there was a discontinuity in reality between God and creation. If symbolism only participated as a copy the ground undergirding symbolic language was washed away.

A Different Framework

A better framework was needed, a framework that would account for both likenesses between God and creatures and the chasm between divine and created being. Thomas Aquinas spent part of his active life constructing such a framework. As a young professor he restated the accepted view that there could be no direct similarity between God and creatures. There was no form, or what might be called a common characteristic or essence, in which both could participate.[81] If religious language was to be grounded in reality, explanations had to be based on some other consideration than a direct likeness.

Nor could symbolic language be grounded in knowing God directly! Thomas was unsympathetic to any suggestion we can have an intellectual intuition of God in this life.[82] Such views ran counter to the basic maxim that in this life normal human experience is drawn ultimately from sense images.[83] Yet religious language does legitimately flow from the corporeal to the divine nature. This could happen only if some likeness could be found which would bridge the gap. Since a direct likeness or a direct intuition was ruled out, the likeness must somehow be indirect.

A theory of analogy suggested itself to Saint Thomas. Analogy implies a relation between things that is indirect, and yet is based on a comparison between two realities. A full discussion of Thomas's notion of analogy is beyond the scope of the present inquiry. However, there are some little noticed texts in his Commentary on the Sentences that deal with analogy and will be useful for our purpose.[84] They are especially interesting because Thomas wrote these when he was a professor at Paris studying the sacraments. He writes,

> In addition to that likeness occurring between things which share the same form [not a suitable option as already noted] there is also a likeness of *proportionality* which involves the juxtaposition of proportions.... This likeness allows us to pass from corporeal things to the divine nature.[85]

What are the advantages of a similarity of proportionality? One advantage is, it does not require any direct comparison be made between things. It is based instead on a comparison of relationships that do not touch on the things themselves. Proportionality is better described as 'relations between relations.' Two examples, doubleness and governance, taken from Saint Thomas will make this clear.[86]

Although, we might not use the word doubleness until we go off to school, it is a simple notion that we become aware of at an early age. It is the simple relationship of Two to One. For example the improper fractions 8/4 and 6/3 embody doubleness. They have a likeness of proportionality because of this. But note that doubleness is not embodied in the terms themselves, that is, in 8 and 6 and 4 and 3.

The second example, governance, is even more apposite to the present purpose. Governance is needed for both a city and a ship. Mayors govern cities while captains govern ships. Mayors who attempted to govern their city like a ship would soon discover it was a failure. Likewise captains cannot govern their ships as a city should be governed. What is clear is that no direct comparison can be made between any of the terms mayors and ships and cities and captains. The style of leadership appropriate in each case cannot be compared. Mayoralties and captaincies are not better or worse examples of leadership; there is no hierarchical relationship. But the notion of governance can be applied to both relationships: as a mayor is to a city: so a captain is to a ship. There is a likeness of proportion between these relationships.

Proportional likeness is useful because it can ground ways of speaking about God without imposing a limitation upon God, nor place God in a category.[87] We might say, "God has a fiery temper and is angry with this generation." This is not symbolic language; it is simply the language of metaphor. Yet the word fire can be applied to God analogously, that is proportionally. Using one of Thomas' examples we could say, that in a forge, fire by its heat has the power to liquefy and improve metal: so God in his goodness has the power through His grace to melt souls and infuse virtue. The liquefying relationship between fire and metal can be compared to the melting relationship between God's grace and the perfected souls of his creatures. Fire and God are not compared in this analogy – that would be metaphor. But the proportion of liquefying to improve and engracing to improve is the subject of comparison.[88]

When analogies are used in sacred histories or in myth cycles listeners can grasp an understanding of what would otherwise be unexplainable.[89] By developing ideas through proportionality it can be seen that although God is truly infinite and creatures are truly finite some things can be said because of a similarity of proportions between them.

Although there can be no direct comparison between the infinite and the finite because the plenitude of the infinite over the finite is not determinable, there can be proportionality between them, i.e. there can be a similarity of proportions. As we relate a finite [thing] to a finite [thing] so we relate an infinite to an infinite.[90]

Using the example of governance again it can be said as mayors are wise in governing their cities for the common good: so God is wise in governing the cosmos for the universal good. The symbolic language has value not because creatures are copies of God, but because both have a relation to Being. Symbolism then speaks in analogous, proportional terms.

Cosmic Analogy

Natural religion becomes possible through analogy. The Creator can be spoken of through the screen of specific objects such as fire, water, wind, totem animals and the like.

In practice it can be seen though, that many of the images formed are at the level of simple metaphor. If bees are busy and industrious, then God is like the bees only busier and more industrious. If Jerusalem is a beautiful city, then heaven is a still more beautiful city. Metaphors are useful, often beautiful and instructive, but they do not talk of God. They speak of creation made perfect. Analogous language is different in that it recognizes the immeasurable differences and uses an indirect comparison.

Natural religions did use the more complex language of symbolism. Careful attention to the lunar month, to the yearly order of the seasons, and to the procession of the equinox required centuries of observation that revealed a steadfast pattern of events. From the rhythms of nature it was possible to form attitudes about the gods who were responsible for them. The patterns suggested faithfulness and stability. If the physical realm exhibited faithful ordering then the notion of faithful ordering would be applicable to the divine nature. The faithful ordering in God would be of a different mysterious character. Through analogy not only can God be conceived as faithful to creation, but also as a Being whose nature is order and faithfulness itself.[91]

Historical Symbolism

Understanding that God is a god who is loyal to the ordering of the seasons as in natural religion is quite different from God's faithfulness in sacred history. That God is faithful to the seed of Abraham, to the particular people of Israel and Judah, and to the Church outlined in the Acts of the Apostles and the Epistles is something different. Sacred history presents God's faithfulness in terms that are more personal and intimate. The language deals with relationships that possessed a completeness that cannot be found through the workings of nature. For example, David a shepherd, the youngest of his clan and without prospects, was remembered by God. He was brought to the king's throne, and despite his infidelities, he was preserved throughout his reign from all his enemies. In this it is possible to see Yahweh the God of sacred history as a God of fidelity and trustworthiness.

Themes reiterated in sacred history constantly proposed fidelity of a particular stamp. In the stories concerning Israel Yahweh's faithfulness seemed to exhibit a gratuitous air. Although God's fidelity to Israel was not destroyed by lapses it was not of the blind variety that condones the lapses. King

David the sinner was restored to favor only upon repentance, and he was still punished for his sins.[92] The myths in Israel's sacred history speak of a fidelity based on a divine justice, a justice that ultimately demands a just response from its human counterpart. Using proportion and not imitation to compare, Divine fidelity is not found to be more while human fidelity is less. The fidelity of God can remain steadfast while human fidelity is breached. Divine and human faithfulness are of two different orders inasmuch as the integrity on which both fidelities were grounded was only similar in a proportional way. This follows logically because the bases to be integrally God and to be integrally human are only analogously alike.

Another theme that can be traced is God's constant attention to the poor. The prophets sent by God regularly paid attention to the downtrodden in the land, and promised reconciliation on condition that Israel repented and began to practice fair dealing and justice. God's message was both compassionate and just. It became an easy step to assume that the God who sent the prophets was something like that.[93]

A philosopher meditating over the possibilities of Being, or studying the cosmos, could not have learned analogies such as these. Awareness came only through of the themes of sacred history.

Sacred history retained its vital importance because it continually revealed the relationships that could be applied to God. The type of fidelity, the range of mercy, the character of divine justice that could be applied to God were derived from sacred history. Correctly interpreted themes of sacred history generated an analogous understanding of the divine way of being. The mythic stories embedded in sacred history fine-tuned the language of cosmic symbolism and moved those who accepted that history beyond the limitations of nature symbolism

Expectations of Religious Symbolism

Even when the notion of analogy is accepted and is adopted as a means for grounding religious symbolism the question still persists, what precisely is communicated by the analogies that one draws between two levels of reality? What is a symbol's referent? Clearly there are some things that analogies do not claim to do! By meditating upon religious symbols the mind does not experience divine illumination. Nor does knowledge of a symbol necessarily generate an experience that is mystical.

What symbols do is otherwise. They orchestrate usual experiences giving them an expanded appreciation and application. Symbols involve drawing comparisons between elements that are not normally at the same level, between elements that are not associated with each other.

The ultimate referent of a symbol is that insight we gain at the instant of seeing the proportional comparison. The objects of our attention are often quite pedestrian, such as captains and ships, mayors and towns; fire and smelting action, water and its cleansing powers. These concrete items, of course, are not the referent of the symbol, but are rather the terms that serve to enable us to grasp a relation. It is the recognition of the proportional likeness found between the terms that is the ultimate referent of the symbol.

Religious symbols, then, do have an objective referent. The referent is the analogous understanding that appears as a result of the juxtaposition of known terms. In this sense the likenesses between God and humanity do have an objective grounding, not in the objects, but in the recognition of proportionality.

Religious symbolism cannot be routinely reduced to simply projections of human aspirations. Simple projections, in other words fantasies about the gods, will always be with us. Not every myth is true. Not every religious myth is true. It is important to be alert so that these do not escape unchallenged.

Ungrounded fantasies tend to meet resistance, not only from the rational analyses, but also in the presence of religious symbols already interiorized by a deeply religious community. Religious fantasy often meets its sharpest critique in the objectivity contained in well-grounded religious symbolism. A meditative mind mulling over the possibilities of divinity within a tradition acquires a skill in drawing proportional comparisons and in rejecting what is bizarre. Those who accept sacred history as a true account of God's activity within the cosmos and toward a given human community, will find an objectivity in that history that will help them shape and ground the meaning of their religious symbolism.

Investigation of the way in which religious symbols become established is well worth undertaking. So also, is an examination of the perseverance and adaptability of particular religious symbols. The continuation of a symbolic expression over many generations, necessarily touching many cultures, will be more than a simple projection of an unmet need. The fact that major world religions have found a home in many different cultures and have at times outlived all the social and economic forces attending their birth points to their being grounded in reality.

What, then, can we expect of religious symbolism communicated to us in myth cycles and in their ritual counterparts? First we should expect that they would use the full range of human experience to point beyond that human experience. They will also orient the homo viator, the pilgrim, in the way in which he or she should go, and will remove something of the strangeness of life's final destination.

In the language of myth symbolism presents a vision of the divinity the content of which is cognitional as well as volitional or emotional. Although obscure, the language is public language. It expresses experiences that can be communicated by one person to another. The comparisons grounded through analogy form the backdrop of all religious understanding — or at least of everyone's potential understanding. But symbols can not tell all, for despite undoubted likenesses they point to, a vast gap remains between creation and the creator. In the final analysis religious symbols are signposts pointing the way to the mystery that is God, to God who necessarily has to remain mysterious in this present life because God's Being exceeds our human ability to grasp.

NOTES

[1] G. S. Kirk, *Myth Its Meaning and Functions in Ancient and Other Cultures* (Cambridge University Press, 1970), 28. Geoffrey Stephen Kirk (1921 – 2003) was a British classical scholar.

[2] Deborah Bird Rose, *Dingo Makes us Human* (Cambridge University Press, 1992), 44. Rose was a consulting anthropologist with the Aboriginal Land Commission and wrote on social and ecological justice issues.

[3] Sir Edward Burnett Tylor (1832-1917) is considered the founder of anthropology in Great Britain. He gave this definition in 1873.

[4] Ernst Cassirer (1874-1945) was a German philosopher whose work deals mainly with how the object of our knowledge and belief comes to be known by us. His thought bore influences from Kant, Herder, and Hegel.

[5] Friedrich Wilhelm Joseph von Schelling (1775-1854) a German Professor who wrote on a wide range of topics. Although he differed from idealist and romantic philosophers, nevertheless he can be counted among those who shared these perspectives.

Georg Wilhelm Friedrich Hegel (1770-1831) a German philosopher. The Hegelian dialectic has been very influential. It postulates a cyclic process in which a thesis is followed by its antithesis resulting in a conflict or dialogue that produces a synthesis, which then becomes a new thesis. Hegelian thought has fueled the idealist movement and the concept of progress so prevalent in academic circles.

[6] Kirk, *Myth*, 263—8.

[7] 1 Sam 24: 1-7.

[8] Jn 1:18

[9] See, Aristotle. 356 b 11

[10] Saint Thomas Aquinas (1224 or 1225-1274) a Dominican theologian. His resolution to the problem of faith and human reasoning was one of the greatest achievements of medieval times. His work continues to have widespread influence. He picks up Saint Paul's distinction. See I Tim ch. 4 lesson 2.

[11] See, The "Myth and Mythology" section of "Genesis" article in *The Anchor Bible Dictionary.* IV:947. And Maurice Wiles, "Myth in Theology" *The Myth of God Incarnate,* Ed. John Hick (SMC Press, 1977), 148-66.

[12] G. D. Kaufman *Systematic Theology, A Historicist Perspective* (NY: Charles Scribner's Sons, 1978), 279-80. Gordon Kaufman (1925-2011) was a noted liberal theologian of the Harvard Divinity School.

[13] See, *Encyclopedia of Religion,* Ed. M. Eliade (NY: Macmillan Publishing Company, 1987), V. 10:506-7.

[14] Quoted from Roland B. Dixon, "Maidu Myths," *Bulletin of the American Museum of Natural History,* xvii 39 Pt. 2, NY, June 30, 1902. pp. 39-40

The Huntington Expedition first gathered Maidu stories in 1902 and published them in 1912 in the publication *American Ethnological Society* Ed., Frank Boaz.

A Maidu man, Maym Benner Galligher, recognized the voice of the speaker in the recordings as that of Tom Young (Hanc'ibyjim) the last of the great Maidu storytellers. See *The Maidu Indian Myths and Stories of Hanc'ibyjim,* Ed., and Trans., William Shipley (Berkeley: Heyday Books 1991). Shipley's book has a somewhat different Maidu origin story. In it two figures, Earthmaker and Coyote, are in a raft looking for earth in a world where there is only water. A small meadowlark's nest came floating on the water. Under Earthmaker's direction Coyote stretches the nest in all four directions until it is

116

big enough to sustain Earthmaker and eventually all other animals. Note that in the Shipley and Dixon accounts, once again, more than one figure is required to form the world.

[15] At the time when this myth was reported, Peheipe played the part of a clown in the dances of the Secret Society.

[16] A full discussion of Genesis would take us too far afield. "The Narrative of Genesis" 5:913-955 and in "Mythology and Bible Study" 4:946-955 in *The Anchor Bible Dictionary* gives a helpful introduction to study to Genesis.

[17] See, Gen 1:1-31

[18] Gen 1: 14-19

[19] See, Gen 1:22

[20] See, Gen 1:26-27

[21] Note, in the Maidu myth there is uncertainty whether men and women will be created at all.

[22] This story was told in a remarkable meeting of an anthropological expedition with the elders of the Arrernte tribe in 1896. W. B. Spencer a professor of anthropology at the University of Melbourne was leader of the party. F. J. Gillen who was also there was a telegraph officer at Alice Springs. Mircea Eliade (1907-1986) a historian of religions who taught in Bucharest and Paris before joining the University of Chicago, makes reference to this Dreaming story in *The Sacred and the Profane* (NY: Harcourt, Brace and World. 1957), 32-33. There is some criticism of Eliade's account. For example, see Jonathan Z. Smith, *To Take Place* (Chicago University Press 1987), 3 et seq. But Eliade's account is still the most accessible.

[23] W. B. Spencer and F. J. Gillen, *The Native Tribes of Central Australia* London, 1899.

---

[24] The term *alchera* is Arrernte, other terms are used in other tribes. For example, the Murrinh-patha refer to *da murntak warra*, the early days, for this period.

[25] Earth-diver forms of creation story also appear outside of North America.

[26] In some North American myths Turtle's role is taken by a bird or animal.

[27] Various Sumerian civilizations are identified in the Middle East between 3000BC and 2000BC. The oral traditions of Sumerian society were committed to writing in the later period.

[28] The relative concentration of the major religions on one or other of major themes is the way in which Huston Smith divides his work in, *The World's Religions*, Revised edition (Harper Collins Publishers, 1991).

[29] See, Joseph Campbell, *The Hero with a Thousand Faces*, Second Edition, [Bollingen Series xvii] (Princeton University Press, 1968).

Joseph Campbell (1904-1987) a professor of literature he was known for his Jungian interpretations of folklore and the role of myth. His interpretation of myth has been criticized by Robert Segel – a topic Segel continually returns to. Segal makes the point that Campbell thought the symbolism to be found in all myths would be universal because myths reveal a universal human nature. Because of this assumption Campbell fails to analyze the plots or the particularity of individual myths to any great extent. See, Robert A Segal, *Joseph Campbell: An Introduction* (Garland Publications, 1987), 137-9.

[30] See, C. G. Jung, *The Archetypes and the Collective Unconscious* [Bollingen Series IX.1] (NY: Princeton University Press, 1959), 3-42, and 157. Carl Gustave Jung (1875-1961) was a Swiss psychiatrist and the founder of analytical psychology.

[31] Stith Thompson has catalogued examples of myths of this type as far away from California as the tribes of America's North East

woodlands in *Motif - Index of Folk Literature* (Bloomington, Indiana: University of Indiana Press, 1966).

[32] Bronislaw Malinowski (2884-1942) Polish born anthropologist. He was trained in philosophy, physics and mathematics. Malinowski became interested in anthropology after reading Frazer's book *The Golden Bough* and later did landmark work in the field.

Sir James George Frazer influential British anthropologist and folklorist (1854-1941). The underlying theme of his seminal work *The Golden Bough* was the evolution of thought from magical to religious to scientific.

[33] Hyemeyohsts Storm, *Seven Arrows* (NY: Ballentine Books, 1973), 17.

[34] Jn 1:18

[35] Mircea Eliade, *The Sacred and Profane*, and *Myth of the Eternal Return* (NY: Harper and Row Publishers, 1971). *Patterns in Comparative Religion* (NY: New American Library, 1963).

[36] Sam D Gill, *Native American Traditions: Sources and Interpretations*, [The Religious Life of Man Series] (Belmont: California, Wadsworth Publishing, 1983).

[37] James Cowan, Mysteries of the Dreaming, Revised Edition. (Linfield, NSW: Unity Press, 1992).

[38] Mary Douglas, *Natural Symbols, Explorations in Cosmology*, (Penguin Books Ltd, 1970).

[39] Adolphus Peter Elkin (1891-1979) professor of anthropology and campaigner for what he regarded as social justice for the Aboriginal people. Elkin is noted for his formation of theory that denied the unity of totemism. His identification of multiple forms of totemisn in Australia was critized by Levi-Strauss.

[40] Eliade, *Myth of the Eternal Return*, 68-69.

[41] *Ibid.*

---

[42] The uniqueness of the historical consciousness of Judaism and Christianity is open to question. See *Encyclopedia of Religion*, 10:284-5.

[43] Current catechesis in the Catholic Church encourages an understanding of the Old Testament and God's relations to the Jews in a program called, The Rite of Christian Initiation for Adults, (RCIA) used when instructing persons for baptism.

[44] See, Michael Shirres, *Te Tagata and The Human Person* (Auckland: Accent Publications, 1997).

[45] Leopold von Ranke (1795-1886) German historian.

[46] See Shakespeare's Macbeth.

[47] Georg Hegel, (1770-1831) German Idealist philosopher.

[48] Karl Heinrich Marx (1818-1883) together with Friedrich Engels produced much of the theory of socialism and communism.

[49] The phrase means many things. For a review see Brevard S. Childs, *Biblical Theology of the Old and New Testaments* (Minneapolis: Fortress Press, 1993).

[50] Max Scheler (1874-1928) German philosopher. See *Encyclopedia of Religion*, 13:96.

[51] Alfred North Whitehead (1861-1947) English scientist and philosopher. Charles Hartshorne (1897-2000) American philosopher, theologian and educator. See Ewert H. Cousins, Ed., *Process Theology Basic Writings* (Newman Press. 1971).

[52] See, *The Myth and Ritual Theory: An Anthology*, Ed. Robert A. Segal (Malden: Mass., Blackwell, 1998).

[53] W. R. Smith, a British biblical scholar, published his theory in the late 1800's. His influence can be seen in the works of Emile Durkheim and Sigmund Freud.

[54] See, Josephine Flood, *Archeology of the Dreamtime* (Pymble, NSW: Collins, Angus and Robertson, 1992).

NOTES

See, Emile Durkheim, *The Primitive Forms of Religious Life*, [reprint of 1915 edition] (NY: Free Press Paperback, 1965), 257 *et seq.*

Eccl. 3: 4-5, 8.

Wolfgang Amadeus Mozart (1756-1791) is widely regarded as the greatest composer who ever lived. Giuseppe Verdi (1813-1868) the foremost composer of Italian romantic opera.

One of Mozart's major works, *The Magic Flute* has been analyzed by Moberley with this in mind.

See, *On Aboriginal Religion* W. E. H. Stanner. [Oceania Monograph No. 11] (Sidney: University of Sydney Press,1964). Stanner gives a design plan for a mythless rite in Chapter 5.

See, Mary Douglas, *Natural Symbols.*

Ernst Cassirer, *Essay on Man* (New Haven: Yale University Press, 1944), 27.

A survey of approaches can be found in Raymond Firth, *Symbols: Public and Private* (London: George Allen & Unwin, 1973).

Emile Durkheim, *Elementary Forms of Religious Life*, [reprint of 1915 edition] (NY: Free Press Paperback, 1965). And Bronislaw Malinowski, *Magic, Science and Religion* (Garden City: Double Day, 1955).

Jn 4:24.

See, The Creed of the Council of Chalcedon (451 AD). This council building on the earlier councils of Nicea in AD 321 and Constantinople in AD 381 expresses a late elaboration of the doctrine of the Incarnation.

See, Moses Maimonides, The Guide for the Perplexed, I:33-5.

Ps. 19 [18]:2.

---

[68] Denis the Pseudo-Areopagite, *Mystical Theology*, PG 3: 997B 16-22. See also "The Uplifting Spirituality of Pseudo Dionysius," *Christian Spirituality: Origins to the Twelfth Century*, eds. McGinn, Meyendorff and Leclercq (NY: Crossroad, 1988), 132-152.

[69] See, Rom 1: 20-21.

[70] Augustine of Hippo (354-430) was one of the foremost philosopher-theologians of early Christianity. He had a profound influence on the development of Western thought.

[71] The distinction appears in Augustine's, *De Triniate*, Bks VI c 10 and XIV ,c. 8. It is cited by Peter Lombard in his Book of *Sentences*, Bk. I, dist. 3. Lombard's *Sentences* became a text used throughout the Medieval Period.

[72] Was the likeness of God found equally in men and women? For a discussion see E. Ann Matter, "Christ, God and Woman in the Thought of Saint Augustine," *Augustine and His Critics*, Eds. R. Dodaro and G. Lawless (London: Routledge, 2000), 164-175.

[73] See, J. Danielou, "The Problem of Symbolism," *Thought* [Fordham University] 25 (1950): 429.

[74] Jn 1:1-2. See also the discussion by Jean Danielou, *Advent of Salvation* (NY: Sheed and Ward, 1950), 39.

[75] Hugo Rahner, *Greek Myths and Christian Mystery* (London: Burns and Oates, 1963).

[76] See, Beryl Smalley, *The Study of the Bible in the Middle Ages*, Third Edition (Oxford: B Blackwell, 1983).

[77] Jude I:3. What was to be included in the canon of Scripture is an issue which came later.

[78] Thomas Aquinas, *Summa Theologica*, I, q.1, a. 10, c. Echoing the point of the Pseudo-Hugh of St. Victor (PL 177:372), also *Summa Theologica* I, q. 85, 1; q. 84, aa. 5 and 6.

[79] See, "Illumination," "Intellectus," and "Mind" in *AugustineThrough the Ages, An Encyclopedia*, Ed., Fitzgerald (Grand Rapids: Eerdmann Publishing, 1999), 438-41; 452-3; 563-67. Also see E Gilson, *The Christian Philosophy of St. Augustine* (NY: Vintage, 1967).

[80] Saint Augustine's presentation is more sophisticated than the simple paraphrase we provide here. The divine ideas are not like mental constructs of humans. For example, they are not plural, and they are not separate from the divine essence.

[81] Thomas Aquinas, *Summa*, I, q. 12, aa. 2 and 4

[82] *Ibid.* I, q. 88, aa. 2 and 3. Mystic visions are another matter, such visions are not universal and not normal means of salvation. Normal means lie in the preached word and the sacraments.

[83] *Ibid.*, I, q 85, a, i.

[84] See, Thomas Aquinas, *Sentences*, Bk. 4, dist., 1, q. 1, a. 1,qla. 5, ad. 3m. similar tests are to be found in Bk. 1 dist. 34, q. 3, a. 1, ad. 2m.

[85] *Ibid.*, Bk. 1, dist. 34, q. 3, a 1, ad. 2m.

[86] *Ibid.*, Bk. 4,dist. 1, q.1,a.1,qla. 5, ad 3m.

[87] *Ibid.*, and Bk. 1, dist. 34, q. 3, a. 1, ad 2m , dist. 1 , q. 1, a.1, qla. 5, ad. 3m.

[88] The same point is made again by Thomas Aquinas with sacramental symbolism. *Sentences*, Bk. 4, dist. 1, q. 1, gla 5, ad 3m.

[89] Statements from a myth cycle can be told to outsiders so they too have an understanding of what is being said and claimed. Outsiders may not accept what is being claimed.

[90] Thomas Aquinas, *Sentences*, Bk. 4, dist. 49, q. 2, a. 1 ad 6m

[91] Jean Danielou makes this point see *op. cit.*, 430-1.

[92] 2 Sam 12:13-17, David eventually regains the Lord's favor, vv. 22-25.

---

[93] Numerous examples can be mentioned, Amos 2:4-8, I Kgs 21:17-28, Jonas 3:1-10, Jer. 35:12-19.

CPSIA information can be obtained at www.ICGtesting.com
Printed in the USA
LVOW090307200312

273879LV00001B/48/P